LIFE TOGETHER STUDENT EDITION

STARTING

TO GO WHERE GOD WANTS YOU TO BE

LIFE TOGETHER STUDENT EDITION

STARTING

TO GO WHERE GOD WANTS YOU TO BE

6 small group sessions
on life together

Doug Fields &
Brett Eastman

lifetogether
student edition

Youth Specialties

ZONDERVAN™

WWW.ZONDERVAN.COM

STARTING to Go Where God Wants You to Be: 6 Small Group Sessions on Beginning Life Together

Copyright© 2003 by Doug Fields and Lifetogether™

Youth Specialties Books, 300 South Pierce Street, El Cajon CA 92020, are published by Zondervan, 5300 Patterson Avenue Southeast, Grand Rapids MI 49530

Library of Congress Cataloging-in-Publication Data

Fields, Doug, 1962-   .
   Starting to go where God wants you to be : 6 small group sessions on
beginning life together / by Doug Fields and Brett Eastman.
          p. cm.
Summary: Provides exercises, readings, and other materials for launching
or revitalizing a small group of teens working together to explore their
relationships with other people and with God.
   ISBN 0-310-25333-0 (pbk.)
   1. Church group work--Juvenile literature. 2.   Small groups--Religious
aspects--Christianity--Juvenile literature. 3.   Teenagers--Religious
life--Juvenile literature. [1. Church group work. 2. Christian life. 3.
Interpersonal relations.] I. Eastman, Brett, 1959- II. Title.
   BV652.2.F53 2003
   259'.23--dc21

                                                                    2003005868

Unless otherwise indicted, all Scripture quotations are taken from the Holy Bible: New International Version (North American Edition). Copyright © 1973, 1978, 1984 by International Bible Society. Used by permission of Zondervan.

Concept and portions of this curriculum are from Doing Life Together (Zondervan, 2002), used by permission from Brett & Dee Eastman, Karen Lee-Thorpe and Denise & Todd Wendorff.

Editorial and Art Direction: Rick Marschall
Production Coordinator: Nicole Davis
Edited: Vicki Newby
Cover and interior design: Tyler Mattson, NomadicMedia.net
Interior layouts, design management, production: Mark Rayburn, RayburnDesign.com
Proofreading: Vicki Newby and Linnea Lagerquist
Design Assistance: Katherine Spencer
Production Assistance: Roni Meek, Amy Aecovalle
Author photos: Brian Wiertzema and Art Zipple

Printed in the United States of America

04 05 06 07 08 09 / DC / 13 12 11 10 9 8

ACKNOWLEDGMENTS

I'm thankful to the adult volunteers at Saddleback Church who are great small group leaders and to the students who are growing spiritually because they're connected to other believers. Good things are happening, and I'm so proud of you!

I'm thankful to the team at www.simplyyouthministry.com for working so hard to help create these types of resources that assist youth ministers and students throughout the world.

Gratitude for help on this project goes to Dennis Beckner, Kathleen Hamer, Erica Hamer, and especially Matt McGill who read every word of each book in the series and has made a big difference in my life and the books I write. What a joy to do life together with friends!

—DF

CONTENTS

READ ME FIRST

Welcome to a relational journey!

My prayer is that this book, a few friends, and a loving adult leader will take you on a journey that will revolutionize your life. The following six sessions were designed to help you grow as a Christian in the context of a caring, spiritual community. This community is a group of people committed to doing life together, at least for a season of your life. Spiritual community is formed when each small group member focuses on Jesus and the others in the group.

Creating spiritual community isn't easy. It requires trust, confidentiality, honesty, care, and commitment to meet regularly with your group. These are rare qualities in today's world. Any two or three people can meet together and call it a group, but it takes something special from you to create a community in which you can be known, be loved, be cared for, and feel safe enough to reveal thoughts, doubts, and struggles and still to be yourself. You may be tempted to show up at the small group session and sit, smile, and be nice, but never speak from your heart or say anything that would challenge another group member's thinking. This type of superficial participation prevents true spiritual community.

Most relationships never get beneath the relational surface. This LIFETOGETHER series is designed to push you to think, to talk, and to open your heart. You'll be challenged to expose some of your fears, hurts, and habits. As you do this, you'll find healing, experience spiritual growth, and build lasting, genuine friendships. Since God uses people to impact people you'll most likely become a richer, deeper, more vibrant person as you experience LIFETOGETHER with others. If you go through this book (and the 5 other books in this series) you will become a deeper and stronger follower of Jesus Christ. Get ready for something big to happen in your life!

WHAT YOU'LL FIND IN EACH SESSION

For each session, the group time contains five sections, one for each of the primary biblical purposes: fellowship, discipleship, ministry, evangelism, and worship. The five purposes can each stand alone, but when they're fused together, they make a greater impact on you and your world than the five of them might if approached separately. Think about it like this: If you play baseball or softball, you might be an outstanding hitter, but you also need to be able to catch, throw, run, and slide. You need more than one skill to make an impact for your team. In the same way, the five purposes individually are good, but when you put them all together, you're a balanced player who makes a huge impact.

The material in this book (and the other LIFETOGETHER books) is built around God's Word. You'll find a lot of blank spaces and journaling pages where you can write down your thoughts about God's work in your life as you explore and live out God's purposes.

Here's a closer look at what you'll find in these five sections:

FELLOWSHIP: CONNECTING Your Heart to Others'
[goal: to have students share about their lives and listen attentively to others]

These questions give you and the members of your small group a chance to share from your own lives, to get to know one another better, and to offer initial thoughts on the session theme. The picture for this section is a heart because you're opening up your heart so others can connect with you on a deeper level.

DISCIPLESHIP: GROWING to Be Like Jesus
[goal: to explore God's Word, learn biblical knowledge, and make personal applications]

This is the time to explore the Bible, gain biblical knowledge, and discuss how God's Word can make a difference in your life. The picture for this section is a brain because you're opening your mind to learn God's Word and ways.

You'll find lots of questions in this section; more than you can discuss during your group time. Your leader will choose the questions your group will discuss. You can respond to the other questions on your own during the week, which is a great way to get more Bible study. (See **At Home This Week** on page 30.)

MINISTRY: SERVING Others in Love
[goal: to recognize and take opportunities to serve others]

During each small group session, you'll have an opportunity to discuss how to meet needs by serving others. As you grow spiritually, you'll begin to recognize—and take—opportunities to serve others. As your heart expands, so will your opportunities to serve. Here, the picture is a foot because you're moving your feet to meet the needs of others.

EVANGELISM: SHARING Your Story and God's Story
[goal: to consider how the truths from this lesson might be applied to our relationships with unbelievers]

It's too easy for a small group to become a clique and only care about one another. That's not God's plan for us. He wants us to reach out to people with the good news. Each session will give you an opportunity to discuss your relationships with unbelievers and consider ways to reach out to them. The picture for this section is a mouth because you're opening your mouth to have spiritual conversations with unbelievers.

WORSHIP: SURRENDERING Your Life to Honor God
[goal: to focus on God's presence]

Each small group session ends with a time of prayer. You'll be challenged to slow down and turn your focus toward God's love, his goodness, and his presence in your life. You'll spend time talking to God, listening in silence, and giving your heart to him. Surrender is giving up what you want so God can give you what he wants. The picture for this section is a body, which represents you surrendering your entire life to God.

AT HOME THIS WEEK

At the end of each session, you'll find reminders of ways you can help yourself grow spiritually until your small group meets again. You're free to vary the options you choose from week to week. You'll find more information about each of these options near the end of the first session.

Daily Bible Readings

Page 104 contains a list of Bible passages to help you continue to take God's Word deeper in your life.

Memory Verses

On page 108 you'll find six Bible verses to memorize, one related to the topic of each session.

Journaling

You're offered several options to trigger your thoughts, including a question or two related to the topic of the session. Journaling is a great way to reflect on what you've been learning or to evaluate it.

Wrap It Up

Each session contains a lot of discussion questions, too many for one small group meeting. So you can think through your answers to the extra questions during the week.

LEARN A LITTLE MORE

You might want to learn a little more (hey, great title for a subsection!) about terms and phrases in the Bible passage. You'll find helpful information here.

FOR FURTHER STUDY

One of the best ways to understand Bible passages is by reading other verses on the same topic. You'll find suggestions here.

BEING IN A SMALL GROUP

You probably have enough casual or superficial friendships and don't need to waste your time cultivating more. To benefit the most from your small group time and to build great relationships, here are some ideas to help you:

Prepare to participate

Interaction is a key to a good small group. Talking too little will make it hard for others to get to know you. Everyone has something to contribute—yes, even you! But participating doesn't mean dominating, so be careful to not monopolize the conversation! Most groups typically have one conversation hog, and if you don't know who it is in your small group, then it might be you. Here's a tip: you don't have to answer every question and comment on every point. The bottom line is to find a balance between the two extremes.

Be consistent

Healthy relationships take time to grow. Quality time is great, but a great *quantity* of time is probably better. Plan to show up every week (or whenever your group plans to meet), even when you don't feel like it. With only six sessions per book, if you miss just two meetings you'll have missed 33 percent of the small group times for this book. When you make a commitment to your small group a high priority, you're sure to build meaningful relationships.

Practice honesty and confidentiality

Strong relationships are only as solid as the trust they are built upon. Although it may be difficult, take a risk and be honest with your answers. God wants you to be known by others! Then respect the risks others are taking and offer them the same love, grace, and forgiveness God does. Make confidentiality a nonnegotiable value for your small group. Nothing kills community like gossip.

Come prepared

You can always arrive prepared by praying ahead of time. Ask God to give you the courage to be honest and the discipline to be respectful of others.

You aren't required to do any preparation in the workbook before you arrive (unless you're the leader—and then it's just a few minutes). But you may want to work through the **Growing** questions before your group time. Talk about this idea with your leader. If your group is going to do this, don't view the preparation as homework but as an opportunity to learn more about yourself and God to prepare yourself to go deeper.

Congratulations...

...on making a commitment to go through this material with your small group! Life change is within reach when people are united through the same commitment. Your participation in a small group can have a lasting and powerful impact on your life. Our prayer is that the questions and activities in this book help you grow closer to the other group members, and more importantly, to grow closer to God.

Doug Fields & Brett Eastman

Doug and Brett were part of the same small group for several years. Brett was the pastor of small groups at Saddleback Church where Doug is the pastor to students. Brett and a team of friends wrote Doing LifeTogether, a group study for adults. Everyone loved it so much that they asked Doug to revise it for students. So even though Brett and Doug both had a hand in this book, it's written as though Doug were sitting with you in your small group. For more on Doug and Brett see page 144.

FOR SMALL GROUP LEADERS

As the leader, prepare yourself by reading through the lesson and thinking about how you might lead it. The questions are a guide for you to help students grow spiritually. Think through which questions are best for your group. No curriculum author knows your students better than you. This small amount of preparation will help you manage the time you'll have together.

How to Go through Each Lesson

This book was written to be more like a guidebook than a workbook. In most workbooks, you're supposed to answer every question and fill in all the blanks. In this book, there are lots of questions and plenty of space.

Rule number one is that there are no rules about how you must go through the material. Every small group is unique and will figure out its own style and system. (The exception is when the lead youth worker establishes a guideline for all the groups to follow. In that case, respect your leader and conform your group to the leader's guidelines).

If you need a standard to get you started until you navigate your own way, this is how we used the material for a 60-minute session.

Intro (4 minutes)
Begin each session with one student reading the **Small Group Covenant** (see page 88). This becomes a constant reminder of why you're doing what you're doing. Then have another student read the opening paragraphs of the session you'll be discussing. Allow different students to take turns reading these two opening pieces.

Connecting (10 minutes)
This section can take 45 minutes if you're not careful to manage the time. You'll need to lead to keep this segment short. Consider giving students a specific amount of time and hold them to it. It's always better to leave students wanting more time for an activity than to leave them tired and bored.

Growing (25 minutes)
Read God's Word and work through the questions you think will be best for your group. This section will usually have more questions than you are able to discuss. Before the small group begins, take time to read through the questions to choose the best ones for your group. You may want to add questions of your own.

Serving and Sharing (10 minutes)
We typically choose one of these two sections to skip if pressed for time. If you decide to skip one or the other, group members can finish the section on their own during the week. Don't feel guilty about passing over a section. One of the strengths of this material is the built-in, intentional repetition. You'll have other opportunities to discuss that biblical purpose.

Surrendering (10 minutes)
We always want to end the lesson with a focus on God and a specific time of prayer. You'll be given several options, but you can always default to your group's comfort level to finish your time.

Closing Challenge (1 minute)
We encourage the students to pick one option from the **At Home This Week** section

that they'll do on their own. The more often students are able to take the initiative and develop the habit of spending time with God, the healthier they will be in their spiritual journey. We've found that students have plenty of unanswered questions that they want to go back and consider on their own.

Keep in Mind

- The main goal of this book isn't to have group members answer every question. The goal is **spiritual growth.**
- Make whatever adjustments you think are necessary.
- It's your small group, it's your time, and the questions will always be there. Use them, ignore them, or assign them to be answered during the week.
- Don't feel the pressure to have everyone answer every question.
- Questions are a great way to get students connecting to one another and God's Word.

Suggestions for Existing Small Groups

If your small group has been meeting for a while and you've already established comfortable relationships, you can jump right into the material. Make sure you take the following actions, even if you're a well-established group:

- Read through the **Small Group Covenant** on page 88 and make additions or adjustments.
- Read the **Prayer Request Guidelines** together (on page 128). You can maximize the group's time by following these guidelines.
- Consider whether you're going to assign the material to be completed (or at least thought through) before each meeting.
- Familiarize yourself with all the **At Home This Week** options that follow each lesson. They are detailed near the end of Session 1 (page 30) and summarized after the other five lessons.

Although handling business like this can seem cumbersome or unnecessary to an existing group, these foundational steps can save you from headaches later because you took the time to create an environment conducive to establishing deep relationships.

Suggestions for New Small Groups

If your group is meeting together for the first time, jumping right into the first lesson may not be your best option. You might want to have a meeting before you begin going through the book so you can get to know each other. To prepare for the first gathering, read and follow the **Suggestions for Existing Groups.**

When you get together with your group members, spend time getting to know one another by using ice-breaker questions. Several are listed here. Pick one or two that will work best for your group. Or you may have ice breakers of your own that you'd like to use. The goal is to break ground in order to plant the seeds of healthy relationships.

Ice Breakers

1. What's your name, school, grade, and favorite class in school? (Picking your least favorite class is too easy.)

2. Tell the group a brief (basic) history of your family. What's your family life like? How many brothers and sisters do you have? Which family members are you closest to?

3. What's one thing about yourself that you really like?

4. Everyone has little personality quirks—strange and unique habits that other people usually laugh about. What are yours?

5. Why did you choose to be a part of this small group?

6. What do you hope to get out of this small group? How do you expect it to help you?

7. In your opinion, what do you think it will take to make our small group work?

Great resources are available to help you!

Companion DVDs are available for the LifeTogether small group books. These DVDs contain teaching segments you can use to supplement each session by playing them before your small group discussion begins or just prior to the Growing to Be Like Jesus discussion. Some of my favorite youth ministry communicators in the world are included on these DVDs. (See page 140.)

In addition to the teaching segments on the DVDs, we've added small group leader tips that are unique to each session. Brett and I give you specific small group pointers and ideas that will help you lead each session. If you spend five to 10 minutes watching the leadership tips and then spend another 10 to 15 minutes reading through each session in advance, you'll be fully equipped to lead students through the material. The DVDs aren't required, but they're a great supplement to the small group material.

In addition, you can find free, helpful tips for leading small groups on our Web site, www.simplyyouthministry.com/lifetogether. These tips are general, so any small group leader may benefit from them.

I encourage you to take advantage of these resources!

What STARTING TO GO WHERE GOD WANTS YOU TO BE is all about

Starting to Go Where God Wants You to Be begins with a call to love God and love others, followed by one session on each of the five biblical purposes: fellowship, discipleship, ministry, evangelism, and worship. It's like a table set with great appetizers. You get to taste them all.

I encourage small groups to begin with **Starting to Go Where God Wants You to Be.** Then study the rest of the books in any order—maybe by interest, maybe in an order that prepares you for events on the youth ministry calendar, such as **Sharing Your Story and God's Story** before an evangelism outreach in the fall or **Serving Others in Love** to prepare for the mission trip in the spring. With five other books to choose from, you're in control. There's no "correct" order for using the books.

You're ready to get started

LIFE TOGETHER STUDENT EDITION

STARTING

TO GO WHERE GOD WANTS YOU TO BE

WHAT ON EARTH AM I HERE FOR?

"Leave me alone!" I said it a million times when I was a teenager. "Leave me alone!" Even though the words came quickly from my lips, aimed at my parents, sisters, and friends, in my heart I didn't feel that way. If I would have been able to identify and express my feelings, I would have said something like this: "I'm lonely! I don't want to go through life without anyone. Don't leave me alone. I need people in my life. Don't believe me when I say, 'Leave me alone.' The more you pay attention to me, the happier I'll be. But I'm afraid to say that I need you. What would I do if you reject me?"

I didn't say what I should have said. Instead I pushed a lot of people away.

Over the years I've learned how to have strong relationships with others—the type that go deeper than the usual superficial level. I've learned plenty of lessons about love and life in these relationships. The more I learn, the better I understand how God created me to be one of the players in a number of relationships—first in relationship with him and then in growing relationships with others. Life hums along at its best when I'm solidly connected to God and people.

The same is true about you. You'll live a deeper, richer, more rewarding life if you can let others get to know the real you. You'll find out how important relationships are to you. No more "leave me alone" cries.

Congratulations for making a commitment to be in a small group. It has the potential to create an environment that enables you to develop strong relationships and to learn about God's purposes for your life. You're about to begin a journey that will give you opportunities to learn more about yourself, others, life, Jesus, and God's Word. What you learn will change you forever.

Begin your journey by committing to reveal the real you. Watch people draw close to you. Life isn't meant to be lived alone. Doing life together is a gift from God.

Let the journey begin.

FELLOWSHIP: CONNECTING Your Heart to Others'

[goal: to have students share about their lives and listen attentively to others]

Everyone hides behind a mask to some degree or another. (Mine is the receding hairline kind of ugly mask.) We naturally don't reveal too much too soon. Little by little, we test the security of our relationships, only revealing private information when we know we're safe.

Ultimately before others can get to know the real you, you have to take some risks to be more open than may feel comfortable. If you stop hiding, you'll be taking the first steps in creating strong relationships. You may not be able to be completely transparent right away, but stretch yourself. You'll find the rewards worth the risks. Besides, you don't expect everyone else to be perfect; others don't expect you to be perfect either. Sometimes our imperfections bond us together the tightest.

Having said that, you won't be able to share for unlimited amounts of time and still get through the entire session. Divide the time allotted among the number of people in the group. Assign someone to watch the time. You'll have many more sessions together to get to know each other better.

As others share their stories, pay attention to what they're saying. Listening carefully when others are talking communicates how much you value them. Active listening is a key skill you'll be developing throughout these sessions.

1
Share information about yourself that will help others know you better—family life, hobbies and interests, the food you hate to eat, animals you hate to pet, what makes you laugh, what makes you smell bad. (You can mix serious information with humorous stuff! Laughing with your small group is a good thing!)

2
Answer the following question with only one sentence: What's the purpose of life?

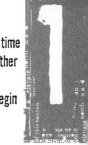

3 If you haven't discussed the **Small Group Covenant** on page 88, take time to read it together and discuss it now. Make commitments to one another that your group time will reflect those values. As a reminder, you may want to have one person read the covenant to the group before you begin each lesson.

Use the **Small Group Roster** (page 90) to record the names and contact information of the small group members.

DISCIPLESHIP: GROWING to Be Like Jesus

[goal: to explore God's Word, learn biblical knowledge, and make personal applications]

Everyone eventually wonders about *the big question.* It can be phrased several ways:

 Are we there yet?

Why am I here?

What's the point?

Does this life matter?

Will I ever go on a date with a human? (Oops! That's an important question, but not the *big* one!)

What's the purpose of life?

It's a natural question, and it's important to pursue answers. Jesus knew that at the core of who you are, you would crave significance and purpose. You need it. That's why Jesus gives the meaning of life in just a few words:

> ³⁴Hearing that Jesus had silenced the **Sadducees,** the Pharisees got together. ³⁵One of them, an **expert in the law,** tested him with this question: ³⁶"Teacher, which is the greatest commandment in the Law?"
>
> ³⁷Jesus replied: " 'Love the Lord your God with all your heart and with all your soul and with all your mind.' ³⁸This is the first and greatest commandment. ³⁹And the second is like it: 'Love your neighbor as yourself.' ⁴⁰All the Law and the Prophets hang on these two commandments."
>
> —Matthew 22:34-40

Terms that look like this are described in Learn a Little More near the end of the session.

What do you know about the Sadducees and the Pharisees? Why would they try to test Jesus? What kind of test was this? (Would you flunk a spelling test if "Sadducee" was on it?)

Reread verse 40. What was Jesus referring to when he says, "all the Law and the Prophets"?

What does Jesus mean when he says, "with all your heart and with all your soul and with all your mind?" How would we put this kind of love into action?

In your own words, what does it mean to love God? Love your neighbor?

Jesus says to "love your neighbor as yourself." What does he mean?

Does every person love himself or herself? Explain your thinking. In what ways do people with low self-esteem still love themselves? What implications do your ideas have about loving others the way Jesus commanded?

STARTING to go where God wants you to be

Jesus answers the legal expert's question with two great commands—the greatest and the second greatest. Is it possible to practice only one command without the other? How would you explain what Jesus means?

10

Do you find these two commands surprising? Why didn't Jesus say, "One of the great commands is to pursue your own happiness"? What are the implications for your life?

11

Which are you better at: loving God or loving others? Explain your answer.

12

What's one extreme act of love you've seen someone else show (either to you or someone else)?

13

MINISTRY: SERVING Others in Love
[goal: to recognize and take opportunities to serve others]

I hope you came to the conclusion that loving God and loving others can't be separated in daily living. Life together with God means life together with others, and life together with others means life with God. God has created a great relational system for us: when we love God, he will give us the power to love others. When we receive love from others, we're thankful to God and learn new ways to increase our love for him.

One of the main points of life on earth is *learning to love*. During the next five lessons in this book, your group will discuss five actions that move you along the path toward loving God and others better. In every lesson you'll be given an opportunity to either discuss ways to show love or you'll be challenged to show love to others in some way. Some lessons will be fairly easy, while other will stretch your comfort zone.

14 Write a definition of what it means to serve others in love.

15 Share your definition with the group. Make notes of ideas others offer that you haven't included in your definition.

16 Take a moment to rewrite your definition, incorporating the best of the ideas shared.

17 What's one practical thing you can do during the coming week to love one of your neighbors better?

EVANGELISM: SHARING Your Story and God's Story

[goal: to consider how the truths from this lesson might be applied to our relationships with unbelievers]

At the beginning of small groups such as this one, you should decide whether your group is open to inviting friends to join your group. If the group is open, answer questions 18-21. Your small group leader or your youth group leadership team may have already determined the group is closed at this time. If so, a good group respects and follows that decision. You may be able to invite friends to join you in the next **LifeTogether** book. If your group is closed now, skip to question 22.

If your group is open at this time

18 Take a few minutes to list names of friends you'll consider inviting to the group's next session.

19 Check the option that seems like the easiest way to invite others to your group. Share your answer.

◇ Call them.
◇ Talk to them at school.
◇ Talk with them when another person from the group is with you.
◇ Send them an e-mail.
◇ Kidnap their pets. Offer to release the pets if they come to your small group. (Okay, maybe not.)
◇ Other _____.

Discuss what might happen if everyone you invite comes to your small group. Could you handle them all? Do you have extra books for everyone? Could you launch another new group? Can someone from your group lead it? What other options do you have? What else do you need to consider?

As you think of some of the potential inconveniences of the new additions, keep in mind God's love for everyone. Love isn't meant to be kept to a few holy, special people. Love is meant to be given away.

Read **How to Keep Your Small Group from Becoming a Clique** on page 92.

If your group isn't open at this time

When is the right time to bring friends to our youth ministry?

How do new people feel when they come into our ministry?

How can each person in our group make new people feel comfortable?

WORSHIP: SURRENDERING Your Life to Honor God
[goal: to focus on God's presence]

Sessions will usually end with prayer. This is your opportunity to submit to God's ways and to connect your heart to God's heart.

Especially if your small group is just beginning, don't feel the pressure to have everyone pray out loud if they're not comfortable with it yet. Group members can pray in the silence of their hearts: "God, help me to be a more loving person. I need help loving _____."

Another option is to close this prayer time by praying for the people whose names you listed on page 27.

You'll find three prayer resources in the back of this book. By reading and discussing them, you'll find your group prayer time more rewarding.

📖 **Praying in Your Small Group** (page 126). Read this article on your own before the next session.

📖 **Prayer Request Guidelines** (page 128). Read and discuss these guidelines as a group.

📖 **Prayer Options** (page 130). Refer to this list for ideas to give your prayer time variety.

Take some time this week to answer the questions on the **Spiritual Health Assessment** (pages 95-103). The goal is to evaluate your spiritual journey honestly, not to get a high score. If you don't have time to write answers for all the questions, make sure you at least circle the numbers on the scale that best apply to you. (It should only take a few minutes.) You may have the opportunity to share your results during your next session.

AT HOME THIS WEEK

Each week, you'll have at least four options to help you grow and learn on your own—which means you'll have more to contribute when you return.

Daily Bible Readings

On page 104 you'll find **Daily Bible Readings,** a chart of Bible passages that correspond with the lessons—five for each week. If you choose this option, read one passage each day. Highlight it in your Bible, reflect on it, journal about it, or repeat it out loud as a prayer. You're free to interact with the Bible verses any way you want. All I'm encouraging you to do is take time to read God's love letter—the Bible. You'll find helpful tips in **How to Study the Bible** (page 105).

Memory Verses

Memorizing Bible verses is an important habit to develop as you learn to grow spiritually on your own. **Memory Verses** (page 108) lists six verses—one per week—for you to memorize if you want to plant God's Word in your heart. Memorizing verses (and making them stick for more than a few minutes) isn't easy, but the benefits are undeniable. You'll have God's Word with you wherever you go.

Journaling

You'll find blank pages for journaling beginning on page 113. At the end of each session, you'll find several options and a question to get your thoughts going—but you aren't limited to the ideas in this book. Use these pages to reflect, to write a letter to God, to note what you're learning, to compose a prayer, to ask a question, to draw a picture of your praise, to record your thoughts. For more suggestions about journaling, turn to **Journaling: Snapshot of Your Heart** (page 110).

Choose one or more questions to reflect on:
- Write about any fears you experienced the last time you took a risk to get to know someone on a deeper level.
- Why do you find it difficult to open up with others?
- What keeps you from loving God like you want to?

Wrap It Up

Write out your answers to the session questions your group didn't have time to discuss.

This week share with the others in your group which option seems most appealing to try during the coming week. During other weeks, take time to share with the group what you did **At Home This Week.**

LEARN A LITTLE MORE

Sadducees, Pharisees, experts in the Law

The *Sadducees* were a politically active group of Jews who were in charge of the temple and its services. They were wealthy aristocrats, descendants of the high-priestly line. They accepted only the Torah (the first five books of the Old Testament) as authoritative. They didn't believe in the resurrection.

Pharisees taught that the way to God was through strict obedience to the law, which included the entire Old Testament and the oral traditions added to it. They exercised great influence over the Jewish people because they controlled the synagogues. Paul, the apostle who wrote most of the New Testament, was a Pharisee at one time.

The *experts in the Law* were experts in the Mosaic Law (the Torah).

These groups often opposed each other because of their differing views, but they united to oppose Jesus because he was a threat to their power, wealth, or prestige. Most people in the Gospels who were opposed to Jesus came from one of these groups.

The first and greatest commandment...and the second

The first commandment is greater because obeying the first—loving God—will lead to the second—loving people. Obedience to the second commandment does not necessarily lead to the first. Many people love other people yet do not love God.

Just because the second command isn't *the* most important doesn't mean the second command is *un*important. A heart that works properly is more important than eyes that work properly, but this doesn't mean we want to live without our eyes.

The Law and the Prophets

A term for the Old Testament.

Neighbor

Sometimes we look for loopholes to excuse us from our responsibilities. A narrow definition of *neighbor* means we have to love only a few people: "Well, that person isn't my neighbor, so I don't have to love him."

According to the parable of the Good Samaritan in Luke 10:25-37, Jesus identifies a neighbor as anyone who crosses our path and has a need. Even if you're not an observant person, you can see that we all have a lot of neighbors to love!

Heart...soul...mind

The precise meanings of these terms overlapped in the Jewish usage. The point Jesus was making emphasizes the call to love God with *every* part of us—emotions, reasoning, imagination, passion, will, energy, and actions. Loving God is not simply an emotion or belief. It extends to the will and to actions.

FOR FURTHER STUDY

Leviticus 19:9-18
Deuteronomy 6:4-5; 10:12-13
Proverbs 4:23
1 John 3:16-18
1 John 4:7-12, 20-21

NOTES

NOTES

CONNECTING YOUR HEART TO OTHERS'

I'll never forget the invitation I received to be part of a small group when I was a ninth grader. I didn't even know what a small group was. I thought our youth group was already pretty small in comparison to other churches, and I didn't understand why we needed to go even smaller. Honestly I was scared. I feared that within a small group I would have to expose my worst thoughts and confess all my sins—neither of which I wanted to do. Forget small. I liked big. I liked hiding. I liked being unknown.

My apprehensions diminished when a twelfth grader made an announcement at my church. He said something like this: "When I was first asked to join a small group, I didn't know what it was all about, and I was a little scared. So if you're scared, I understand. All I can say is that my small group experience has changed my life. Trust me. You won't regret it if you get involved in one."

Wow! I felt understood. God knew what I needed to hear. He used that senior to say to me, "Doug, do it. Trust me." I did.

Now, 30 years later I can say to others, "My small group experiences have changed my life. Trust me. Get connected with other Christians. Your life will be changed." One of my life's highlights has been watching my own children get involved in small groups and grow. (I'm still waiting to hear their worst thoughts and sins though.)

The life impact from participating in small groups is no secret to those who encouraged you to join. They know what happens: God's people—Christians—will influence and impact other Christians. It's a great design. When God is working in one life, he uses it to influence another life.

You're in for a unique journey. You may not yet recognize what God will do in your life through the others sitting around you. And you may be surprised to learn that God will use *you* to help them.

May your lives influence one another for godliness as you grow closer together.

FELLOWSHIP: CONNECTING Your Heart to Others

Last time you all were together, you started off by sharing a little about your life story. Now deepen your connection with one another by sharing your spiritual story. Regardless of where you're at on your spiritual journey, you have something to share. Don't feel pressure to say you've made it to certain road markers if you haven't gotten there. Let your group get to know the real you.

If you need help getting started, answer one or more of the following questions:

1 What's your current interest in spiritual things?

2 Who do you respect who seem to have a close relationship with God? What seems different about them?

3 Describe your relationship with God.

4 What makes it tough for you to live out your faith?

5 When was the first time you heard that God loves you? How did you respond to that? How does his love make a difference in your everyday life?

DISCIPLESHIP: GROWING to Be Like Jesus

God has designed us to be connected with him and with other people. This passage from Hebrews describes how these two connections ought to impact one another.

> ²³Let us hold unswervingly to the hope we profess, for he who promised is faithful. ²⁴And let us consider how we may spur one another on toward love and good deeds. ²⁵Let us not give up meeting together, as some are in the habit of doing, but let us encourage one another—and all the more as you see the Day approaching.
>
> —Hebrews 10:23-25

6 Hope (verse 23) means wanting something to happen but not being able to control whether it does. What do Christians hope for?

7 Verse 23 also says, "for he who promised is faithful." Do Christians put hope in God's promises or do they put faith in God's promises? What's the difference between hope and faith?

8 This passage says we ought to spur one other on. Where should you be spurring your friends to?

9 How might you spur on another believer in your life?

When you're with your friends, do they see that you have faith in God? Rate yourself on a scale of one (no one sees my faith ever) to ten (others can almost see God walking everywhere with me). Explain your thinking—especially if you give yourself a 13.

What do you think it means to have a "spiritual friend-ship?"

How often do you talk about spiritual ideas or events with your friends? Do you talk about spiritual things with them outside of a church program or small group?

What are some common barriers that keep people from becoming close friends? Why is it that lots of people have many acquaintances but few deep friendships—or none?

How do your friendships influence your relationship with God? Do they help or hinder? Explain your answers.

How can you begin or maintain the habit of meeting with other Christians as verse 25 describes? How can your small group members help you?

STARTING to go where God wants you to be

15 Is it okay to not be part of a church or small group? Why shouldn't we all just worship God alone?

16 How can worshiping God alongside other believers become more important and helpful to you?

 # MINISTRY: SERVING Others in Love

One of the benefits of a small group is being with like-minded friends (as opposed to no-minded friends) who are on a spiritual journey similar to yours. Sometimes we just need companionship for areas of life that feel too risky to take on alone. For example, you might think God wants you to care for an elderly neighbor, but you're too scared to walk into a convalescent hospital by yourself. If a friend joins you, you're likely to find it much easier. After a while, you'll feel like you can go on your own, but it's nice to have a friend who will help get you started.

17 Share something that you've always wanted to do for others but haven't done yet. The reason you haven't done it can be anything, not just fear.

18 Would you be more likely to get started if you didn't have to do it alone?

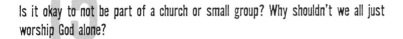

As the others in your group answer this question, you may feel prompted to say, "I'll do that with you." If you feel this way, say it—or at least tell the person later.

EVANGELISM: SHARING Your Story and God's Story

How can a group of fun, committed friends be an evangelistic presence on a school campus? How might strong friendships be a testimony to those who don't know God?

Disneyland offers entertainment. The church offers relationships. Which do you think is more attractive to an unbelieving teenager? Why?

WORSHIP: SURRENDERING Your Life to Honor God

Thanking God for your friendships in the group is a great way to focus on the main point of this week's study—God uses people to impact people. Use one of the journal pages in the back of this book to write a short prayer of praise for one person in your group. You don't have to make it public. You don't have to tell what or who you wrote about. You don't even have to write the person's name on the page.

Finishing up by thanking God for your friends in the group is a great way to focus on the main point of this week's study—God uses people to impact people. After a few minutes, stop writing and pray together.

Get back together with the group. Pray a prayer of thanksgiving for each person in the small group, something as simple as, "God I want to thank you for _____. Now I'll be a better person because of [him or her]." The prayer is simply an acknowledgment that doing life together is one of the ways you'll grow closer to God.

If your small group wants to further study the importance of getting connected, Connecting Your Hearts to Others, another book in the LifeTogether series, is what you're looking for. It contains six lessons dealing primarily with God's purpose of fellowship.

AT HOME THIS WEEK

Choose one or more of the following options.

Daily Bible Readings
Check out the Scriptures on page 104.

Memory Verses
Try memorizing a verse from page 108.

Journaling
- Write whatever is on your mind.
- Read your journal entry from last week and write a reflection on it.
- Respond to this question: *How would it feel to be totally known by the others in your small group?*

Wrap It Up
Write out your answers to the session questions your group didn't have time to discuss.

LEARN A LITTLE MORE

Background: the curtain

 Therefore, brothers, since we have confidence to enter the Most Holy Place by the blood of Jesus, by a new and living way opened for us through the curtain, that is, his body, and since we have a great priest over the house of God, let us draw near to God with a sincere heart in full assurance of faith, having our hearts sprinkled to cleanse us from a guilty conscience and having our bodies washed with pure water.

—Hebrews 10:19-22

The book of Hebrews refers to the Old Testament more than any other New Testament book, which can make it difficult for us to understand. This passage refers to the tabernacle (which later became the temple), a special place where God was present so the Israelites could worship him. This place was also called the Tent of Meeting because God met with his people there.

God is so holy that the people weren't allowed directly into God's presence. Our imperfection can't exist there. Only the priests came close to God's presence. Their job was to go to God on behalf of the people. Thick curtains prevented them from entering the most holy place of the time.

Once Jesus died on the cross, he became the perfect High Priest who made it possible for the entire world to have direct access to God's presence. Many of us have difficulty understanding (and even appreciating) exactly what this means.

Perhaps this example from our lives will help. Think about a bank vault and the employees who work at the bank. You can go inside the bank but you can't go into the vault. Only the employees can go in and out of the vault on behalf of the customers. Imagine if the bank president were to unlock all the bank doors, turn off the alarms, and open the vault so you could have access to the money whenever you want, any time of the day or night. You might consider yourself set for life!

I feel a little uneasy comparing the ancient worship in the tabernacle with going to the bank. (It's a little too much like reality for some.) Still, in Christ we have unlimited access to God and the riches of his grace. Access wasn't always available, but now we can stand confidently in God's presence because of what Jesus has done for us.

FOR FURTHER STUDY

Hebrews 13:1-5
Titus 3:8-11
2 Peter 3:10-1
1 Peter 1:22-2:1
Acts 2:42-47
Matthew 18:20
1 Thessalonians 5:14-15

NOTES

GROWING TO BE LIKE JESUS

I began working with junior high students in 1979. As I write this book I'm still working with teenagers in a local church. Over the years, I've seen thousands of students come and go. Throughout the years, I've learned some of the basic reasons students come to church: parents force them, cute boys or cute girls are there, free donuts, cute boys or girls eating donuts, interest in spiritual things, an invitation from a friend, and getting to go to camp.

The reasons students stop attending church tend to be more varied. Those who leave the church and "fall away" from their relationship with God are usually the ones who attended church but never learned how to grow spiritually on their own. This isn't always the case, but many students discover that showing up at church and growing spiritually are not the same thing.

Because a lot of the guys in my youth group are into lifting weights, I'm always thinking about ways the gym relates to—illustrates—the Christian life. I have a gym membership, but I hate working out there. Pumping weights is hard work that doesn't come naturally to me. Sitting in the sauna is much more natural. My favorite reason for going to the gym is because they have a little café that sells great smoothies and incredible sandwiches. I meet friends at the gym all the time, never for weight training, occasionally to sit in the sauna, and always for food. As a result, I have little muscles and a growing waistline. That reminds me of some Christians I know. They're spiritually flabby with a notable absence of spiritual muscle.

Spiritual growth happens when you work together with God. God does the impossible (gives you a new life and changes your heart), and you do the possible. Being connected to God and growing closer to him often involve actions that don't seem natural—spending time alone, silence, reading the Bible, praying, meditating, thinking, listening. Sitting with friends and drinking smoothies is a lot more fun.

Are you willing to learn how to become spiritually fit? If you are, you'll need encouragement and help from your small group. This lesson is like a trip to the gym. This time forget the food and the sauna and hit the weights.

FELLOWSHIP: CONNECTING Your Heart to Others'

Share something you've done recently that has helped you grow spiritually. How did it help? Was it easy or difficult or somewhere in between? Could you do it every day?

Who is someone—a man or woman—you respect because of his commitment to God? How long has he been a follower of Jesus? How much effort do you guess he has put into his spiritual growth? (Maybe you could ask him this week.) What can you learn from him?

 # DISCIPLESHIP: GROWING to Be Like Jesus

People who have learned to grow spiritually on their own have developed some habits. Jesus reveals that one of the secrets to spiritual growth is being connected to God through prayer and the Word. Mature Christians spend time with God through both.

¹"I am the Real Vine and my Father is the Farmer. ²He cuts off every branch of me that doesn't bear grapes. And every branch that is grape-bearing he prunes back so it will bear even more. ³You are already pruned back by the message I have spoken.

⁴"Live in me. Make your home in me just as I do in you. In the same way that a branch can't bear grapes by itself but only by being joined to the vine, you can't bear fruit unless you are joined with me.

⁵"I am the Vine, you are the branches. When you're joined with me and I with you, the relation intimate and organic, the harvest is sure to be abundant. Separated, you can't produce a thing. ⁶Anyone who separates from me is deadwood, gathered up and thrown on the bonfire. ⁷But if you make yourselves at home with me and my words are at home in you, you can be sure that whatever you ask will be listened to and acted upon. ⁸This is how my Father shows who he is—when you produce grapes, when you mature as my disciples."

—John 15:1-8 *The Message*

Why does Jesus call himself the vine?

What does Jesus mean when he tells us to live in him (verse 4)?

What are some common obstacles or barriers that keep you from living in Jesus?

What does it mean to bear grapes? Why does Jesus want you to bear grapes?
- Is bearing grapes simply being a good witness for Christ? Doing the right things?
- If bearing grapes means doing good deeds, then how can this passage say, "Separated, you can't produce a thing?" Does this mean non–Christians can't do good deeds?
- How does verse 8 help answer this question?

What are some examples in your own life of bearing grapes?

As the branch draws nourishment from the vine, so we ought to draw spiritual nourishment from Christ. How well do you do living in Jesus?

What are some practical ways of living in Jesus?

What would it look like if you were to make yourself at home with Jesus and if his words were at home in you (verse 7)?

One key to drawing nourishment from Jesus is simply time, time to focus your mind on him. On page 104 you'll find **Daily Bible Readings**, a list of Bible passages that you can read or study each day.

This is a good week to read **How to Study the Bible** (page 105).

If you're already spending personal time with God on a consistent basis, try something new to deepen your relationship with God. Learning new habits helps you grow spiritually on your own.

- Memorize a verse (see **Memory Verses** on page 108).
- Write your prayers on a journaling page at the back of this book.
- Get quiet for an extended time of silence with a spiritual focus (not sleep!).

MINISTRY: SERVING Others in Love

Many people find reading the Bible difficult. They've read Genesis several times, maybe even the beginning of Exodus. But they can't seem to get past the instructions and rules in the next few books—especially the ones about sacrificing chickens, goats, and hippos. It's so confusing to read and hard to understand.

Think about the gym illustration. If it's not natural and easy, we typically don't want to do it. Staying connected to God through his Word is one of the ways we grow spiritually, so it's important even though it's often difficult.

11

What can your small group do to help others in your youth ministry read the Bible?

As you list some possible answers, consider whether one of them could be starting a new small group that helps others understand the Bible. What a ministry that would be!

12

If you were to take the challenge to live in Jesus—to grow closer to him and learn his words (the Bible)—how would your ability to serve others be impacted? In other words, what's the connection between being connected to God and helping others?

Take a moment to consider your motives for helping others. Is it possible to bear grapes with the wrong motives? Peel grapes for the wrong person? In light of today's passage, what significance do your motives hold for how you serve others?

EVANGELISM: SHARING Your Story and God's Story

Is your church a place where you feel comfortable bringing your non-Christian friends?
- If yes, when was the last time you brought someone to church?
- If no, what can you do to make the church a place where you'd feel comfortable bringing them?

When was the last time you had a spiritual conversation with an unbeliever? Why do some people avoid talking about spiritual things?

WORSHIP: SURRENDERING Your Life to Honor God

Read John 15:1-8 again. Turn to a journal page in the back of this book and rewrite the passage in your own words.

After everyone is finished, have a few people read their paraphrases as a way of closing in prayer. Be brave about volunteering! This is a way to let others get to know you better.

3

If your small group wants to further study the importance of growing spiritually, Growing to Be Like Jesus, another book in the LifeTogether series, is what you're looking for. It contains six lessons dealing primarily with God's purpose of discipleship.

AT HOME THIS WEEK

Choose one or more of the following options.

Daily Bible Readings
Check out the Scriptures on page 104.

Memory Verses
Try memorizing a verse from page 108.

Journaling
Use **SCRIBBLE** pages, 113-125
- Write whatever is on your mind.
- Read your journal entry from last week and write a reflection on it.
- Respond to these questions: *What habits do I need to develop to grow spiritually on my own? Why is there such a big emphasis on "on your own" in this session?*

Wrap It Up
Write out your answers to the session questions your group didn't have time to discuss.

LEARN A LITTLE MORE

The Real Vine
Studying imagery in Scripture can be challenging. Without even meaning to, we can easily read into the illustration and "find" truths or principles that God doesn't intend. Even highly competent scholars disagree on interpretations occasionally. You may want to do some research in reference books (such as commentaries, study Bibles, or Bible dictionaries) and with knowledgeable teachers to better understand Jesus' teaching in John 15.

FOR FURTHER STUDY

Hebrews 12:5-11
2 John 9
1 John 2:28; 3:17
Psalm 15

NOTES

NOTES

Congratulations! You're gifted." I like to tell the students at my church that. Most teenagers can point out *other* gifted students at their school or describe the talents of their friends, but rarely do they consider themselves gifted. How about you? Do you consider yourself gifted? Do you think you have strong abilities? A unique personality? Experiences that have helped you encourage others?

Even if you don't think so, you *are* gifted. I hope I'm not the first one to inform you of this fact. You may not believe it yet, but everyone I've ever met is a combination of weaknesses and strengths. Everyone has some strengths. No one is perfect, and no one is a total loser (even though you might be tempted to shout out a few names of people you believe fit that category).

As you study the Bible, you'll discover that God gives all Christians gifts—spiritual gifts—to discover and develop to use and to build up the church. No Christian gets every spiritual gift God has to offer. Why? Because you're too imperfect for that! You need to benefit from the gifts of others in order to live life to its fullest. God wants to do great things in your life, and he uses other people to help make that happen. You contribute to them, and they add to the depth of your life.

The leader of your small group will help you discover your gifts and encourage you to use them. My prayer is that the time your group has together today will be an eye-opening experience about how God has uniquely shaped you.

Congratulations! You're gifted too!

FELLOWSHIP: CONNECTING Your Heart to Others'

Choose one of the following questions to answer.

What's one thing you love to do that makes you smile because you're good at it?

What's one area of your life people tell you you're good at? Why might they think that?

What do you think is one of your spiritual gifts? (If you have no idea what spiritual gifts are, answer a different question!) Why do you think so?

 # DISCIPLESHIP: GROWING to Be Like Jesus

You're an original masterpiece God has shaped to live for him and serve him. He's given you gifts, abilities, and passions in a combination that no other person has exactly as you do..

Jesus told a story to explain to his followers about serving. Read this passage one or two times as a group and work through the following questions.

 14"Again, [God's kingdom] will be like a man going on a journey, who called his servants and entrusted his property to them. 15To the one he gave five talents of money, to another two talents, and to another one talent, each according to his ability. Then he went on his journey. 16The man who had received the five talents went at

STARTING to go where God wants you to be

once and put his money to work and gained five more. [17]So also, the one with the two talents gained two more. [18]But the man who had received the one talent went off, dug a hole in the ground and hid his master's money.

[19]"After a long time the master of those servants returned and settled accounts with them. [20]The man who had received the five talents brought the other five. 'Master,' he said, 'you entrusted me with five talents. See, I have gained five more.'

[21]"His master replied, 'Well done, good and faithful servant! You have been faithful with a few things; I will put you in charge of many things. Come and share your master's happiness!'

[22]"The man with the two talents also came. 'Master,' he said, 'you entrusted me with two talents; see, I have gained two more.'

[23]"His master replied, 'Well done, good and faithful servant! You have been faithful with a few things; I will put you in charge of many things. Come and share your master's happiness!'

[24]"Then the man who had received the one talent came. 'Master,' he said, 'I knew that you are a hard man, harvesting where you have not sown and gathering where you have not scattered seed. [25]So I was afraid and went out and hid your talent in the ground. See, here is what belongs to you.'

[26]"His master replied, 'You wicked, lazy servant! So you knew that I harvest where I have not sown and gather where I have not scattered seed? [27]Well then, you should have put my money on deposit with the bankers, so that when I returned I would have received it back with interest.

[28]" 'Take the talent from him and give it to the one who has the ten talents. [29]For everyone who has will be given more, and he will have an abundance. Whoever does not have, even what he has will be taken from him. [30]And throw that worthless servant outside, into the darkness, where there will be weeping and gnashing of teeth.' "

—Matthew 25:14-30

Have someone from your group retell this parable in his or her own words.

4

Who do the characters represent?

5

Why does the man give each servant a different amount of money?

6

Was the servant who had more talents better than the others? Why or why not?

7

What does the money represent? What does it mean when the servant with five talents "put his money to work and gained five more"?

8

Using our gifts to build up the kingdom makes God happy. Describe a time when God used you to make a positive impact in someone else's life.

Verse 19 reads, "After a long time the master of those servants returned and settled accounts with them." Do you ever think about settling accounts with God? What runs through your mind? How does the idea of settling accounts with God change your perspective on life?

What's the main point of this parable? How does that challenge you personally?

Why was the master angry with the servant who had been given one talent?

What warning does this parable give?
What does it mean?

What are some responsibilities, gifts, or resources God has given you? Name five qualities you like about yourself.

MINISTRY: SERVING Others in Love

15

Rate each of the following statements with a 1, 2, or 3. Don't ponder them. Go with your first reaction.

> 1. That's me—I could do that and enjoy it.
> 2. I'm not sure—I might be okay with that.
> 3. Not me—I'd rather be kicked in the head.

_____ Plan a party to celebrate when we finish this book.

_____ Make sure visitors feel welcome when they attend youth group meetings or activities.

_____ Call small group members who have missed a meeting.

_____ Remind people of upcoming events.

_____ Organize parents to help drive for small group activities.

_____ Raise a bunch of money and send it to the authors of this book.

_____ Share something during the next meeting about what you've learned from your personal Bible reading.

_____ Lead the Bible study part of your next meeting—or the whole thing.

_____ Create several Bible study tools to help others learn to read and study their Bible.

_____ Coordinate a service project this group can tackle.

_____ Invite a friend to join the group when you start the next **LifeTogether** book.

_____ Talk with a friend who doesn't attend church programs or events about spiritual ideas.

_____ Build a submarine out of toothpicks.

_____ Lead the opening or closing prayer time in your next meeting.

_____ Help group members learn to grow spiritually, on their own, when the group isn't meeting together.

If you had to choose one—only one—of the above activities as your first-choice activity, which would you pick?

As a group, how can you confirm each other's choices? Sometimes it's difficult to see your own strengths. It helps to have others say, "Oh, I think you're very strong at _____." It might be worth some discussion if you see that one of the group members is missing something.

How can you and the other group members use your first-choice answers to contribute to the health of your small group?

EVANGELISM: SHARING Your Story and God's Story

The Bible teaches that our gifts are to build up the body of Christ (the church), but that doesn't mean our gifts are ineffective outside the church. Look at the following list of gifts and discuss ways you can use them to reach out to non-Christians.

teaching

prayer

service and mercy

hospitality

wisdom

encouragement

generosity

evangelism

If you want to know more about spiritual gifts, read these passages.

Romans 12:6-8
1 Corinthians 12:4-11; 28-30
Ephesians 4:7,8,11,12
1 Peter 4:9-11

WORSHIP: SURRENDERING Your Life to Honor God

Take some time to be silent. While you're quiet, ask God for the wisdom to be able to understand the spiritual gifts he has given you. During this time, consider making a commitment to God that you will study the Scriptures dealing specifically with spiritual gifts.

Close your time in prayer. Be specific and pray in thanks-giving for one another. ("God, thank you for Chad. You've gifted him to be an encourager...")

If your small group wants to further study the importance of connecting through service, **Serving Others in Love**, another book in the LifeTogether series, is what you're looking for. It contains six lessons dealing primarily with God's purpose of ministry to others.

AT HOME THIS WEEK

Choose one or more of the following options.

Daily Bible Readings
Check out the Scriptures on page 104.

Memory Verses
Try memorizing a verse from page 108.

Journaling
Use SCRIBBLE pages, 113-125
- Write whatever is on your mind.
- Read your journal entry from last week and write a reflection on it.
- Respond to these questions: *How am I gifted? What can I do with my gifts?*

Wrap It Up

Write out your answers to the session questions your group didn't have time to discuss.

LEARN A LITTLE MORE

To the one he gave five talents of money, to another two talents, and to another one talent

Even though the master gave each servant a different amount of money, he expected them all to be equally faithful, and he rewarded fairly. The reward was proportional to the demand.

Talents

A talent is a unit of measurement, weighing somewhere between 60 and 80 pounds. Even one talent was a considerable amount. Understanding this makes the master's attitude interesting. In verse 21, the master calls the five talents a few things—in other words, a little amount. It seems he was more interested in the faithfulness of the servants than the bottom line.

You are a hard man

The master was serious about his business. He wasn't angry with the unfaithful servant because he hadn't made a large amount of money with it. He was angry because he never even tried.

God has given all of his children gifts. They aren't for making money, of course! We're to be faithful to use what he has given, using our gifts to bring glory to God and build his kingdom. A day of reckoning will come, and we will either be rewarded or punished for how we use the gifts we've been given.

FOR FURTHER STUDY

1 Peter 4:10
1 Corinthians 12:1-31; 14:26

NOTES

SHARING YOUR STORY AND GOD'S STORY

My high school–aged daughter loves to watch the Entertainment Channel. Her favorite shows are the ones in which the host leads the viewers through a countdown of the 25 most attractive whatever—most attractive actors, dresses, lips, hair pieces, nasal cavities. You name it—they show it. If I'm walking by the television, I'll throw out my opinion or we'll comment on the judge's selections. You might hear us make observations like these:

"Oh, she's not that pretty, is she, Dad?"

"Oh yeah, she's beautiful, but the guy who came in at number 5 is too old to be the best looking, right?"

"Oh no, Dad. He may be old, but he's still hot."

"Really? Old and hot. Am I as handsome as he is?"

"Seriously? Not a chance!" [followed by gagging noises].

We have fun, but the judging process is superficial.

The last time we watched this show, we had a great conversation about what *really* makes someone attractive. It didn't take long before we moved from looks to character and actions. Even though we're different in age and have different friends and experiences, we were both wise enough to know that whether someone is hot has little to do with true quality.

Have you ever considered that people who don't know Jesus are judging how you live your life as a Christian? Your life is sending a message to the viewing audience members who watch from their unbelieving seats. Most non-Christians I talk to aren't turned off by Jesus. They're turned off by Christians. Sad, but true. Many Christians never reveal the attractiveness that a life filled with the Holy Spirit has.

When was the last time you stopped long enough to evaluate the message you're sending? How would non-Christians rank your character? Would they see any difference between your life and the life of non-Christian friends? Do you care?

The reason it's worth caring about and discussing is because, before you share about God's story, people want to know that God's story has changed you. Even if they don't realize it, they're watching to see if you're being genuine and honest about your life. The story you tell must be backed up by your lifestyle.

 # FELLOWSHIP: CONNECTING Your Heart to Others'

1 Finish this sentence: "When my peers look at my life, I want them to see a person who is..."

2 Describe what you think most non–Christians believe about the Christians at your school.

 # DISCIPLESHIP: GROWING to Be Like Jesus

A monk who lived during the Middle Ages, St. Francis of Assisi, made a well-known observation: "Preach the gospel at all times. Use words if necessary." Talk without action is unconvincing. People don't care about God's story if they don't feel like the storyteller—that's you!—cares about them.

Jesus made this point by comparing his followers to light in a dark world. When you shine, people notice.

¹⁴"You are the light of the world. A city on a hill cannot be hidden. ¹⁵Neither do people light a lamp and put it under a bowl. Instead they put it on its stand, and it gives light to everyone in the house. ¹⁶In the same way, let your light shine before men, that they may see your good deeds and praise your Father in heaven."

—Matthew 5:14-16

3 This passage makes it clear that Christians are light in a dark world. What did Jesus mean when he implied that the world is without light? Is it still a dark world today?

4 Do people who live in a dark world—unbelievers—consider themselves to be in the dark? If not, how might you help people see this?

Although Christians are the light of the world and lights can't be hidden, why do most Christians struggle to have spiritual conversations with non-Christians? **5**

6 What does it mean to let your light shine?

7 How can good deeds make an impact on the lives of unbelievers? What actions can you take to help others know God? Be as specific as possible.

8 Who is one person—not yet a Christian—you might have a conversation with next week about spiritual ideas? How might you bring up the topic?

9 What do you think about this statement: Sometimes Christians do good deeds so others praise them rather than praising God.

10 If you had just a few minutes to share the essential ideas about what it means to be a Christian, what would you say?

11 This passage was originally written in Greek. In the original language we can tell *you* is plural. (*You* singular and *you* plural are the same word in English.) God doesn't intend for you to be a light by yourself. How can your family or your small group be lights together?

MINISTRY: SERVING Others in Love

Jesus told his followers in John 13:35, people "will know that you are my disciples, if you love one another." Jesus didn't mention the depth of our Bible knowledge, the length of our perfect church attendance record, our Christian T-shirts, or bumper stickers. Love reveals our master.

12 What are ways a light-bearing Christian can show love on a daily basis? Brainstorm a list, even if the idea is basic. Even "lowly" acts of service reflect God's love.

EVANGELISM: SHARING Your Story and God's Story

Being called to be the light of the world is both a privilege and responsibility. Consider for a minute what it would look like to be a light in your world, your community, your school, your work environment, your neighborhood, your home, and your extended family.

13 List some ways that you might be able to be an attractive light in the following places:

at home   at school   at work   on your team

If your small group were to have an all-night party that included games, food, videos, laughs, and plain old hanging around, what would an unbeliever observe about your group? What might be attractive? What might send a negative message?

If an unbelieving friend asked, "Why are you a follower of Jesus?" what would you say? Your answer to this question is the foundation of your testimony—the story of God's work in your life.

If that same friend asked, "Why would God want a relationship with me?" what would you say? Your answer to this question may begin to form some of the elements of God's story. Do you know how you might explain God's story?

WORSHIP: SURRENDERING Your Life to Honor God

Break into pairs. Share with your partner one area from your life that negatively impacts your witness that you need to pay closer attention to (language, bad attitude, cheating...).

Pray for one another, including prayers for the areas you've just shared.

If your small group wants to further study the importance of reaching out and drawing others in, Sharing Your Story and God's Story, another book in the LifeTogether series, is what you're looking for. It contains six lessons dealing primarily with God's purpose of evangelism.

AT HOME THIS WEEK

Choose one or more of the following options.

Daily Bible Readings
Check out the Scriptures on page 104.

Memory Verses
Try memorizing a verse from page 108.

Journaling
Use **SCRIBBLE** pages, 113-125
- Write whatever is on your mind.
- Read your journal entry from last week and write a reflection on it.
- Respond to this question: *What needs to change in my life so I become a brighter light to others?*

Wrap It Up
Write out your answers to the session questions your group didn't have time to discuss.

LEARN A LITTLE MORE

The light of the world
To best understand this passage is to connect the word *light* with good deeds. All Christians are called to be a light in this world, and the way that we shine is through our actions, more specifically, obedience to God's Word. It's not enough to simply *do* the right things. We should do the right things with right attitudes so that non-Christians might praise God rather than praise us. Our willingness to do the right thing with the right attitude will be tested repeatedly throughout our lives.

Background: lamp

"The small wicker oil lamps of this period gave little light in the average home, which had few windows; they would be most effective by being set on a lamp stand. Something large placed over them would presumably extinguish the light altogether."

From The IVP Bible Background Commentary: New Testament by C. S. Keener (InterVarsity Press, 1993).

Background: salt

This lesson focused on being light, but one verse earlier, Jesus uses another illustration on the same topic: salt.

Jesus uses the imagery of salt and light to describe the kind of influence the community of believers ought to have in the world. One commentator notes: "Jesus' followers would be like salt in that they would create a thirst for greater information."* The context best explains the meaning: salt ought to maintain its saltiness, and Christians ought to maintain their example of being Christ-like. Christians are the light of the world because we reflect the light of Christ. Verse 16 indicates our good deeds are the light we bring into the world. The purpose of light is to be seen and grant sight, not to be hidden so that the world remains lost in the darkness.

* From The Bible Knowledge Commentary by J. F. Walvoord and others (Victor Books, 1987).

FOR FURTHER STUDY

Ephesians 2:10; 5:1-2
1 Peter 2:12
Acts 4:13

NOTES

NOTES

SURRENDERING YOUR LIFE TO HONOR GOD

Every Monday night is family night at my house. All five of us take turns choosing what we'll do as a family. We can pick anything within reason—bowling, shopping, movies, whatever. I typically choose some food option because I like to go out to eat. My oldest daughter regularly requests that we stay at home and play board games.

I hate to admit this in writing, but this is my least favorite option. I hate to lose at the games we play, which is what typically happens. Actually, because I know my kids will read this book with their small group, I'd better admit the truth: I always lose. It doesn't matter what we play—Connect Four, Mad Gab, Go Fish, Dad Is a Dork, Anyone Can Win This Game but Doug, anything. I always lose. I can't count how many times I've said, "I give up." It's become a joke in my house, "Let's guess how long we can play before Dad says, 'I give up.' "

I've become an expert at saying, "I give up," during board games, but I'm still a novice when it comes to saying it to God. As I continue to grow in my faith, I've got to get better at regularly giving up—surrendering—my life so God can fill me up. This is tough because surrender involves losing. Losing control of those things that keep me from focusing more clearly on God.

Surrender is a lifelong struggle for everyone. That's why the word *journey* is a good description of our relationships with God. Everything doesn't happen overnight. Even learning to worship him takes time. Worship is more than singing. It involves surrendering self and lifting up God. John the Baptist said it well. "[Jesus] must become greater; I must become less" (John 3:30). That's worship! Worship is the topic today. Encourage one another to become winners by giving up.

FELLOWSHIP: CONNECTING Your Heart to Others

1 What do you think of when you hear the word *surrender*?

2 Share one area of your life where you need to become less in order for God to become more.

DISCIPLESHIP: GROWING to Be Like Jesus

God created you to worship. We usually find it easier to worship things than God. Worshiping God requires constant surrendering of your life. Daily, we face a vicious fight to ignore the dazzling but empty objects that command our attention and draw our focus away from God.

While it can be difficult, surrender is possible. The Bible is filled with heroes who encountered God and refused to worship anything other than the Creator. Worship is linked to surrender and these two actions are seen in Jesus' encounter with a man and a woman:

> [36]Now one of the Pharisees invited Jesus to have dinner with him, so he went to the Pharisee's house and reclined at the table. [37]When a woman who had lived a sinful life in that town learned that Jesus was eating at the Pharisee's house, she brought an alabaster jar of perfume, [38]and as she stood behind him at his feet weeping, she began to wet his feet with her tears. Then she wiped them with her hair, kissed them and poured perfume on them.
> [39]When the Pharisee who had invited him saw this,

he said to himself, "If this man were a prophet, he would know who is touching him and what kind of woman she is—that she is a sinner."

40Jesus answered him, "Simon, I have something to tell you."

"Tell me, teacher," he said.

41"Two men owed money to a certain moneylender. One owed him five hundred denarii, and the other fifty. 42Neither of them had the money to pay him back, so he canceled the debts of both. Now which of them will love him more?"

43Simon replied, "I suppose the one who had the bigger debt canceled."

"You have judged correctly," Jesus said.

44Then he turned toward the woman and said to Simon, "Do you see this woman? I came into your house. You did not give me any water for my feet, but she wet my feet with her tears and wiped them with her hair. 45You did not give me a kiss, but this woman, from the time I entered, has not stopped kissing my feet. 46You did not put oil on my head, but she has poured perfume on my feet. 47Therefore, I tell you, her many sins have been forgiven—for she loved much. But he who has been forgiven little loves little."

48Then Jesus said to her, "Your sins are forgiven."

49The other guests began to say among themselves, "Who is this who even forgives sins?"

50Jesus said to the woman, "Your faith has saved you; go in peace."

—Luke 7:36-50

What motivated this woman to honor Jesus in this way?
Why might she have been moved to tears?

In this passage we see the Pharisee judge both Jesus and the woman. She must have felt very uncomfortable entering the house of a Pharisee and hearing what he was saying about her.

- Have you ever let the opinions of others negatively influence your worship of God?
- Have your opinions or judgments ever kept someone from experiencing God? (This may be harder to admit. Be brave!)

Look back at verse 47. What does Jesus mean?

Do some people have more sins to be forgiven than others? If this is true, does this mean that some people, those with fewer sins, will never have a chance to love much?

This woman gave up valuable perfume to honor Christ. What do you value that you want to offer God? It doesn't have to be a material possession, just something valuable. Be as specific as possible.

Simon, the Pharisee who questioned Jesus, had a huge blind spot. He was judgmental of the woman for her sins, yet he didn't acknowledge his own. Do you have a hard time seeing your own faults? What are some faults you think you might have (maybe because someone told you)?

STARTING to go where God wants you to be

Surrendering your life to God requires you to acknowledge your personal faults and ask for God's forgiveness. Do you make a conscious effort to confess your imperfections and sins to God regularly? What would help you keep a clean record with God?

When you experience God's mercy and forgiveness in your life, how do you feel? What happens when you try to avoid acknowledging your sins and asking God for forgiveness?

The interaction between the woman and Jesus ends with a gift of peace, something we can reasonably assume the woman lacked before she entered the party. Is your life blessed with peace from your circumstances? Peace from God? Explain why or why not. If not, what keeps you from experiencing peace?

MINISTRY: SERVING Others in Love

Many Christians have a limited definition of worship. They hear the word *worship* and think only of singing. But singing is just one element of what it means to worship God. The Bible refers to several activities that can be thought of as worship:

- LIVING (Romans 12:1)
- PRAYING (Psalm. 95:6)
- HEARING the Word (John 17:17; Deuteronomy 31:11)
- GIVING (1 Corinthians 16:1-2)
- BAPTIZING (Romans 6:3-4)
- MEDITATING (Joshua 1:8)
- SILENCE (Habakkuk 2:20)
- CELEBRATING the Lord's Supper (1 Corinthians 11:23-26)

How might your small group be able to increase awareness of worship? How can you help each other promote worship as a lifestyle of surrender to God on a regular basis? Make a list of ideas.

Who in your small group is interested in taking the lead with one or more of your ideas?

 # EVANGELISM: SHARING Your Story and God's Story

In the second chapter of Acts, new Christians were filled with the Holy Spirit and began speaking in languages they didn't know. People who didn't know what was happening were amazed, while some mocked them and thought they were drunk (see verses 12-13). Even today when people observe acts of genuine worship, some are amazed at God's power, and some mock Christians.

Read the following quotation out loud. What's your response?

> The response of the crowd at Pentecost was mixed. Some mocked the apostles, while others were amazed at what they heard. It doesn't seem as though God was put off by the scoffing. He added 3,000 people to his kingdom that day. The connection between worship and evangelism seemed to work back then.
> —From Purpose-Driven Youth Ministry by me (Doug).

14 Is it possible for genuine worship to be connected to evangelism? If so, how? If not, why?

WORSHIP: SURRENDERING Your Life to Honor God

The woman in Luke 7 surrendered herself in a way that was confusing and troublesome to Simon. Her desire to be at the feet of Jesus was so important that she did what may have been unusual and uncomfortable. Often those are feelings that accompany worship.

15 Now that you've been meeting for several weeks, I hope your group has established a level of trust that enables you to risk sharing about personal issues. End your meeting time by taking a risk: share something that's keeping you from growing spiritually. It could be a problem, a hurt, a habit, or a frustration. Remember the unusual and uncomfortable feeling the woman must have experienced.

16 Close your time together in group prayer. Choose someone else in the group to pray for. Consider laying hands on one another and praying for one another as a sign of commitment and unity.

If your small group wants to further study the importance of worship, Surrendering Your Life to Honor God, another book in the LifeTogether series, is what you're looking for. It contains six lessons dealing primarily with God's purpose of worship.

WHAT'S NEXT?

Do you agree to continue meeting together? If yes, continue on with the remaining questions.

Five other books in the **LifeTogether** series help you establish God's purposes in your life. Discuss which topic your group will study next.

Connecting Your Heart to Others' : 6 Small Group Sessions on Fellowship

Growing to Be Like Jesus: 6 Small Group Sessions on Discipleship

Serving Others in Love: 6 Small Group Sessions on Ministry

Sharing Your Story and God's Story: 6 Small Group Sessions on Evangelism

Surrendering Your Life to Honor God: 6 Small Group Sessions on Worship

You might have noticed this study guide, **STARTING to Go Where God Wants You to Be**, contained one session on each topic.

17 Turn to the **Small Group Covenant** (page 88). Do you want to change anything in your covenant—time, date, shared values, and so on? Write down the changes you agree upon. (Transfer them into your next **LifeTogether** book.)

18 This is a good time to make suggestions for other changes—starting on time, paying attention when others are sharing, rotating leadership responsibilities, or whatever ideas you have—for improving the group.

AT HOME THIS WEEK

Choose one or more of the following options.

Daily Bible Readings
Check out the Scriptures on page 104.

Memory Verses
Try memorizing a verse from page 108.

Journaling
Use **SCRIBBLE** pages, 113-125
- Write whatever is on your mind.
- Read your journal entry from last week and write a reflection on it.
- Respond to this question: *How am I affected when I worship God?*

Wrap It Up
Write out your answers to the questions your group didn't discuss.

LEARN A LITTLE MORE

Reclined
During the time of Jesus, guests commonly dined while lying on their sides, propped up on one elbow. Jesus' feet were stretched out.

Alabaster jar of perfume
"Alabaster jars were carved, expensive, and beautiful. Such jars were made from a translucent, compact gypsum, carved with a long neck that was to be broken off when the contents were poured out. This jar held an expensive perfume. Many Jewish women wore a small perfume flask on a cord around their neck. This jar of perfume would have been valued very highly by this woman." —**From the Life Application Commentary Series CD-ROM (Livingstone, 2000).**

She wiped [Jesus' feet] with her hair, kissed them and poured perfume on them
The woman initially only intended to wipe the perfume on Jesus' feet, but she began to cry. Her tears fell on his feet, so she wiped them with her hair. Her weeping was probably a sign of deep remorse over sin. For a woman to unbind her hair in public was scandalous, and kissing someone's feet was beyond shocking. The whole display had overtones of illicit love.

She is a sinner
The Pharisees, one of the religious groups of the Jews, had a tendency to emphasize moral purity. At times, this was expressed by a strong avoidance of the people who were considered to be "sinners." Sadly some Christians today still hold this hypocritical attitude.

Five hundred denarii...fifty
Both of these debts were huge, as a single denarius was a day's wage. This story isn't about the amount of sin, but rather one's self-awareness of sin.

FOR FURTHER STUDY

Romans 3:23; 5:8; 6:23
Isaiah 1:18
Psalm 32
James 4:6-10
Ephesians 2:1-5

NOTES

If you are watching the LIFETOGETHER DVD, you may use this page to take notes.

NOTES

APPENDIXES

SMALL GROUP COVENANT

Read through the following covenant as a group. Discuss concerns and questions. You may modify the covenant based on the needs and concerns of your group members. Those who agree with the terms and are willing to commit themselves to the covenant as you've revised it should sign their own books and the books of everyone entering into the covenant.

> A covenant is a binding agreement or contract. God made covenants with Noah, Abraham, and David, among others. Jesus is the fulfillment of a new covenant between God and his people.

If you take your commitment to the Small Group Covenant seriously, you'll find that your group will go deep relationally. Without a covenant you may find yourselves meeting simply for the sake of meeting.

If your group decides to add some additional values (character traits such as be encouraging or be kind), write the new values at the bottom of the covenant page. Your group may also want to create some small group rules (actions such as not interrupting when someone else is speaking or sitting up instead of lying down). You can list those at the bottom of the covenant page also.

Reviewing your group's covenant, values, and rules before each meeting will become a significant part of your small group experience.

OUR COVENANT

I, _Angeline. A._ , as a member of our small group, acknowledge my need for meaningful relationships with other believers. I agree that this small group community exists to help me deepen my relationships with God, Christians, and other people in my life. I commit to the following:

Consistency I will give my best effort to attend every time our small group meets.

Honesty I will take risks to share truthfully about the personal issues in my life.

Confidentiality I will support the foundation of trust in our small group by not participating in gossip. I will not reveal personal information shared by others during our meetings.

Respect I will help create a safe environment for our small group members by listening carefully and not making fun of others.

Prayer I will make a committed effort to pray regularly for the people in our small group.

Accountability I will allow the people in my small group to hold me accountable for growing spiritually and living a life that honors God.

This covenant, signed by all the members in this group, reflects our commitment to one another.

Angeline .K. A	_05/30/05_
Signature	Date
(signature)	_05/30/05_
Signature	Date
Joana Bay	_May 30, 06_
Signature	Date
Robelle	
Signature	Date
Signature	Date
Signature	Date
Signature	Date
Signature	Date
Signature	Date
Signature	Date

SMALL GROUP
Roster

name	EMAIL

Phone	Address	school & GRADE

HOW TO KEEP YOUR SMALL GROUP FROM BECOMING A CLIQUE

Cliques arise naturally because we all want to belong—God created us to be connected in community with one another. The same drive that creates community creates cliques. A clique isn't just a group of friends, but a group of friends uninterested in anyone outside the group. Cliques result in pain for those who are excluded.

If you reread the first paragraph of the introduction "**Read Me First**" (page 9), you see the words *spiritual community* used to describe your small group. If your small group becomes a clique, it's an *unspiritual* community. You have a clique when the biblical purpose of fellowship turns inward. That's ugly. It's the opposite of what God intended the body of Christ to be.

- Cliques make your youth ministry look bad.
- Cliques make your small group appear immature.
- Cliques hurt the feelings of excluded people.
- Cliques contradict the value God places on each person.
- Few things are as unappealing as a youth ministry filled with cliques.

Many leaders avoid using small groups as a means toward spiritual growth because they fear the groups will become cliquish. But when they're healthy, small groups can improve the well-being, friendliness, and depth of your youth ministry.

> Be wise in the way you act toward outsiders; make the most of every opportunity.
>
> —Colossians 4:5

Here are some ideas for preventing your small group from turning into a clique:

Be Aware

Learn to recognize when people feel like they don't fit in with your group. It's easy to forget when you're an insider how bad it feels to be an outsider.

Reach Out

Once you're aware of a person feeling left out, make efforts to be friendly. Smile, shake hands, say hello, ask them to sit with you or your group, and ask simple yet personalized questions. A person who feels like an outsider may come across as defensive, so be as accepting as possible.

Launch New Small Groups

Any small group that has the attitude of "us four and no more" has become a clique. A time will come when your small group should launch into multiple small groups if it gets too big. The bigger a small group gets, the less healthy it will become. If your small group understands this, there will be a culture of growth instead of cliques. New or introverted people often are affected by cliques because they have a hard time breaking through the existing connections that the small group members already have. When you start new groups you'll see fellowship move from ugly to what God intended—a practical extension of his love.

Challenge Others

Small group members expect adult leaders to confront them for acting like a clique. Instead of waiting for an adult to make the move, shock everyone by stepping up and challenging what you know is destructive. Take a risk. Be a spokesperson for your youth ministry and your student peers by leading the way—be part of a small group that isn't cliquey and one who isn't afraid to challenge the groups who are.

By practicing these key ideas, your group will excel at reaching out to others and deepening the biblical fellowship within your church.

ACCOUNTABILITY QUESTIONS

During your small group time, you'll have opportunities to connect with one other person in the group—your spiritual partner. Relationships can go deeper if you have the same partner for the entire book or even the entire LIFETOGETHER series. Be as mellow as you want or crank it up to a higher level by talking throughout the week and checking in with each other about your spiritual journeys.

For those who want to go to a deeper level with their spiritual partners, here's a list of questions you can use as a guide for accountability. Depending on the time you have available, you might discuss all of them or only a couple.

The Wonder Question
Have you maintained an attitude of awe and wonder toward God?
(Have you minimized him? Placed him in a box? Forgotten to consider his character?)

The Priority Question
Have you maintained a personal devotional time (quiet time) with God?
(Have you allowed yourself to become too busy? Filled your life with too much activity?)

The Morality Question
Have you maintained integrity in the way you live?
(Have you compromised your integrity or the truth with your actions? Your thoughts? Your words?)

The Listening Question
Are you sensitive to the promptings and leading of the Holy Spirit?
(Have you drowned out his voice with too much noise?)

The Relationships Question
Have you maintained peaceful relationships and resolved conflicts to the best of your ability? (Have you caused conflict, offended others, or avoided resolving tension?)

The Prayer Question
How can I pray for you this week?

SPIRITUAL HEALTH assessment

Evaluating your spiritual journey is a good thing. Parts of your journey will take you to low spots, while others will lead you to high places. Spiritual growth is not a smooth incline—loopy roller coaster is more like it. When you regularly consider your life, you'll develop an awareness of God's Spirit working in you. Evaluate. Think. Learn. Grow.

The assessment in this section is a tool, not a test. The purpose of this tool is to help you evaluate where you're at in your faith journey. No one is perfect in this life, so don't worry about what score you get. It won't be published in your church bulletin. Be honest so you have an accurate idea of how you're doing.

When you finish, celebrate the areas where you're relatively healthy, and think about how you can use your strengths to help others on their spiritual journeys. Then think of ways your small group members can aid one another to improve weak areas through support and example.

 FELLOWSHIP: CONNECTING Your Heart to Others'

1. I meet consistently with a small group of Christians.

1	2	3	4	5
poor				outstanding

2. I'm connected to other Christians who hold me accountable.

1	2	3	4	5
poor				outstanding

3. I can talk with my small group leader when I need help, advice, or support.

1	2	3	4	5
poor				outstanding

4. My Christian friends are a significant source of strength and stability in my life.

1	2	3	4	5
poor				outstanding

5. I regularly pray for others in my small group between meetings.

1	2	3	4	5
poor				outstanding

6. I have resolved all conflicts I have had with other Christians and non-Christians.

1	2	3	4	5
poor				outstanding

7. I've done all I possibly can to be a good son or daughter and brother or sister.

1	2	3	4	5
poor				outstanding

Take time to answer the following questions to further evaluate your spiritual health (after your small group meets if you don't have time during the meeting). If you need help with this, schedule a time with your small group leader to talk about your spiritual health.

8 List the three most significant relationships you have right now. Why are these people important to you?

9 How would you describe the benefit you receive from being in fellowship with other Christians?

Do you have an accountability partner? If so, what have you been doing to hold each other accountable? If not, how can you get one?

DISCIPLESHIP: GROWING to Be Like Jesus

11. I have regular times of conversation with God.

1	2	3	4	5
poor				outstanding

12. I'm a closer friend with God this month than I was last month.

1	2	3	4	5
poor				outstanding

13. I'm making better decisions this month when compared to last month.

1	2	3	4	5
poor				outstanding

14. I regularly attend church services and grow spiritually as a result.

1	2	3	4	5
poor				outstanding

15. I consistently honor God with my finances through giving.

1	2	3	4	5
poor				outstanding

16. I regularly study the Bible on my own.

1	2	3	4	5
poor				outstanding

17. I regularly memorize Bible verses or passages.

1	2	3	4	5
poor				outstanding

Take time to answer the following questions to further evaluate your spiritual health (after your small group meets if you don't have time during the meeting). If you need help with this, schedule a time with your small group leader to talk about your spiritual health.

What books or chapters from the Bible have you read during the last month?

What has God been teaching you from Scripture lately?

What was the last verse you memorized? When did you memorize it? Describe the last time a memorized Bible verse helped you.

 # MINISTRY: SERVING Others in Love

21. I am currently serving in some ministry capacity.

1	2	3	4	5
poor				outstanding

22. I'm effectively ministering where I'm serving.

1	2	3	4	5
poor				outstanding

23. Generally I have a humble attitude when I serve others.

1	2	3	4	5
poor				outstanding

24. I understand God has created me as a unique individual and he has a special plan for my life.

1	2	3	4	5
poor				outstanding

25. When I help others, I typically don't look for anything in return.

1	2	3	4	5
poor				outstanding

26. My family and friends consider me to be generally unselfish.

1	2	3	4	5
poor				outstanding

27. I'm usually sensitive to the hurts of others and respond in a caring way.

1	2	3	4	5
poor				outstanding

Take time to answer the following questions to further evaluate your spiritual health (after your small group meets if you don't have time during the meeting). If you need help with this, schedule a time with your small group leader to talk about your spiritual health.

If you're currently serving in a ministry, why are you serving? If not, what's kept you from getting involved?

What spiritual lessons have you learned while serving?

What frustrations have you experienced as a result of serving?

EVANGELISM: SHARING Your Story and God's Story

31. I regularly pray for my non–Christian friends.

   1   2   3   4   5
   poor   outstanding

32. I invite my non–Christian friends to church.

   1   2   3   4   5
   poor   outstanding

33. I talk about my faith with others.

   1   2   3   4   5
   poor   outstanding

34. I pray for opportunities to share about what Jesus has done in my life.

   1   2   3   4   5
   poor   outstanding

35. People know I'm a Christian by more than my words.

   1   2   3   4   5
   poor   outstanding

36. I feel a strong compassion for non–Christians.

   1   2   3   4   5
   poor   outstanding

37. I have written out my testimony and am ready to share it.

   1   2   3   4   5
   poor   outstanding

Take time to answer the following questions to further evaluate your spiritual health (after your small group meets if you don't have time during the meeting). If you need help with this, schedule a time with your small group leader to talk about your spiritual health.

Describe any significant spiritual conversations you've had with unbelievers in the past month.

38

Has your faith been challenged by any non-Christians? If yes, how?

39

What have been some difficulties you've faced with sharing your faith?

40

41

What successes have you experienced recently in personal evangelism? (Success isn't limited to bringing people to salvation directly. Helping someone take a step closer at any point on his or her spiritual journey is success.)

WORSHIP: SURRENDERING Your Life to Honor God

42. I consistently participate in Sunday and midweek worship experiences at church.

1	2	3	4	5
poor				outstanding

43. My heart breaks over the things that break God's heart.

1	2	3	4	5
poor				outstanding

44. I regularly give thanks to God.

1	2	3	4	5
poor				outstanding

45. I'm living a life that, overall, honors God.

1	2	3	4	5
poor				outstanding

46. I have an attitude of wonder and awe toward God.

1	2	3	4	5
poor				outstanding

48. I use the free access I have into God's presence often.

1	2	3	4	5
poor				outstanding

Take time to answer the following questions to further evaluate your spiritual health (after your small group meets if you don't have time during the meeting). If you need help with this, schedule a time with your small group leader to talk about your spiritual health.

49

Make a list of your top five priorities. You can get a good idea of your priorities by evaluating how you spend your time. Be realistic and honest. Are your priorities in the right order? Do you need to get rid of some or add new priorities? (As a student you may have some limitations. This isn't ammo for dropping out of school or disobeying parents!)

List ten things you're thankful for.

50

51

What influences, directs, guides, or controls you the most?

DAILY BIBLE READINGS

As you meet together with your small group friends for Bible study, prayer, and encouragement, you'll grow spiritually. No matter how deep your friendships go, you're not likely to be together for your entire lives, so you need to learn to grow spiritually on your own too. God has given you an incredible tool to help—his love letter, the Bible. The Bible reveals God's love for you and gives directions for living life to the fullest.

To help you, you'll find a collection of Bible passages that reinforce each week's lesson below. Every day *read* the daily verses, *reflect* on how the verses inspire or challenge you, and *respond* to God through prayer or by writing in your journal or on the journaling pages in this book.

Check off the passages as you read them. Don't feel guilty if you miss a daily reading. Simply do your best to develop the habit of being in God's Word daily.

☐ Week 1
Jeremiah 29:11
Philippians 3:7-11
Matthew 5:13-16
2 Corinthians 4:16-18
John 1:12-14

☐ Week 2
Ephesians 2:18-20
Romans 12:4-6
Genesis 1:27-28
Matthew 5:23-24
John 13:35

☐ Week 3
Luke 6:43-45
Luke 6:46-49
1 Peter 2:2-3
Psalm 119:165
Matthew 5:6

☐ Week 4
Galatians 6:9-10
Acts 9:32-42
Philippians 2:19-22
Exodus 35:20-29
Matthew 25:37-40

☐ Week 5
Acts 1:8
John 13:35
Matthew 13:1-9
Matthew 13:18-23
Matthew 9:35-38

☐ Week 6
Romans 12: 1-2
1 Peter 2:4-5
Luke 1:26-38
Genesis 22:1-18
Matthew 5:8

HOW TO STUDY THE BIBLE

The Bible is the foundation of all the books in the LIFETOGETHER series. Every lesson contains a passage from the Bible for your small group to study and apply. To maximize the impact of your small group experience, it's helpful if each participant spends time reading and studying the Bible during the week. When you read the Bible for yourself, you can have discussions based on what *you* know the Bible says instead of what another member has heard second- or third-hand about the Bible. You also minimize the risk of depending on your small group for all your Bible study time.

Growing Christians learn to study the Bible on their own so they can learn to grow on their own. Here are some principles about studying the Bible to help you give God's Word a central place in your life.

Choose a Time and Place

Since we're so easily distracted, pick a time when you're at your best. If you're a morning person, then give that time to study the Bible. Find a place away from phones, computers, and TVs, so you are less likely to be interrupted.

Begin with Prayer

Make an effort to acknowledge God's presence. Thank him for his gifts, confess your sins, and ask for his guidance and understanding as you study his love letter to you.

Start with Excitement

We easily take God's Word for granted and forget what an incredible gift we have. God wasn't forced to reach out to us, but he did. He's made it possible for us to know him, understand his directions, and be encouraged, all through the Bible. Remind yourself how amazing it is that God wants you to know him.

Read the Passage

After choosing a passage, read it several times. You might want to read it slowly, pausing after each sentence. If possible, read it out loud. Originally the Bible was heard, not read.

Keep a Journal

Respond to God's Word by writing down how you're challenged, truths you want to remember, thanksgiving and praise, sins to confess, commands to obey, or any other thoughts you have.

Dig Deep

When you read the Bible, look deeper than the plain meaning of the words. Here are a few ideas about what you might find.

Truth about God's character
What do the verses reveal about God's character?

Truth about your life and our world
You don't have to figure out life on your own. Life can be difficult, but when you know how the world works you can make good decisions guided by wisdom from God.

Truth about the world's past
The Bible reveals God's intervention in our mistakes and triumphs throughout history. The choices we read about—good and bad—serve as examples to challenge us to greater faith and obedience. (See Hebrews 11:1-12:1.)

Truth about our actions
God will never leave you stranded. Although he allows us to go through hard times, he is always with us. Our actions have consequences and rewards. Just like he does in Bible stories, God can use all of the consequences and rewards caused by our actions to help others.

As you read, ask these four questions to help you learn from the Bible:

📖 What do these verses teach me about who God is, how he acts, and how people respond?

- What does this passage teach about the nature of the world?
- What wisdom can I learn from what I read?
- How should I change my life because of what I learned from these verses?

Ask Questions

You may be tempted to skip over parts you don't understand, but don't give up too easily. Understanding the Bible can be hard work. If you come across a word you don't know, look it up in a regular dictionary or a Bible dictionary. If you come across a verse that seems to contradict another verse, see whether your Bible has any notes to explain it. Write down your questions and ask someone who has more knowledge about the Bible than you. Buy or borrow a study Bible or check the Internet. Try these sites to begin with:

www.twopaths.com
www.gotquestions.org
www.carm.org

Apply the Truth to Your Life

The Bible should make a difference in your life. It contains the help you need to live the life God intended. Knowledge of the Bible without personal obedience is worthless and causes hypocrisy and pride. Take time to consider the condition of your thinking, attitudes, and actions, and wonder about how God is working in you. Think about your life situation and how you can serve others better.

More Helpful Ideas

- Take the position that the times you have set aside for Bible reading and study are nonnegotiable. Don't let other activities squeeze Bible study time out of your schedule.
- Avoid the extremes of being ritualistic (reading a chapter just to mark it off a list) and lazy (giving up).
- Begin with realistic goals and boundaries for your study time. Five to seven minutes a day may be a challenge for you at the beginning.
- Be open to the leading and teaching of God's Spirit.
- Love God like he's your parent (or the parent you wish you had).

MEMORY VERSES

The word *memory* may cause some people to throw this book and kick the dog. Throughout your school years, you have to memorize dates, places, times, and outcomes. Now we're telling you to memorize the Bible?! Seriously?

Not the entire Bible. Start with some key verses. Here's why: Scripture memorization is a good habit for a growing Christian to develop. When God's Word is planted in your mind and heart, it has a way of influencing how you live. King David understood this when he wrote; " I have hidden your word in my heart that I might not sin against you" (Psalm 119:11).

Challenge one another in your small group to memorize the six verses below—one for each time your small group meets. Hold each other accountable by asking about one another's progress. Write the verses on index cards and keep them handy so you can learn and review them when you have free moments (standing in line, before class starts, when you've finished a test and others are still working, waiting for your dad to get out of the bathroom…). You'll be surprised at how many verses you can memorize as you work toward this goal and add verses to your list.

WEEK 1

Love the Lord your God with all your heart and with all your soul and with all your strength.

—Deuteronomy 6:5

WEEK 2

"For where two or three come together in my name, there am I with them."

—Matthew 18:20

STARTING to go where God wants you to be

Week 3

I have been crucified with Christ
and I no longer live, but Christ lives
in me. The life I live in the body,
I live by faith in the Son of God,
who loved me and gave himself for me.

—Galatians 2:20

Week 4

For we are God's workmanship
created in Christ Jesus to do good works,
which God prepared in advance
for us to do.

—Ephesians 2:10

Week 5

"For we cannot help
speaking about
what we have seen and heard."

—Acts 4:20

Week 6

Come,
let us bow down in worship,
let us kneel
before the Lord our Maker.

—Psalm 95:6

JOURNALING: SNAPSHOTS OF YOUR HEART

In the simplest terms, journaling is reflection with pen in hand. A growing life needs time to reflect, so several times throughout the book you're asked to reflect in writing and you always have a journaling option at the end of each session. Through these writing opportunities, you're getting a taste of what it means to journal.

When you take time to write reflections in a journal, you'll experience many benefits. A journal is more than a diary. It's a series of snapshots of your heart. The goal of journaling is to slow down your life to capture some of the great, crazy, wonderful, chaotic, painful, encouraging, angering, confusing, joyful, and loving thoughts, feelings and ideas that enter your life. Writing in a journal can become a powerful habit when you reflect on your life and how God is working.

You'll find room to journal on the following pages.

Personal Insights

When confusion abounds in your life, disorderly thoughts and feelings can become like wild animals. They often loom just out of range, slightly out of focus, but never gone from your awareness. Putting these thoughts and feelings on paper is like corralling and domesticating the wild beasts. Then you can look at them, consider them, contemplate the reasons they were causing you pain, and learn from them.

Have you ever had trouble answering the question, "How do you feel?" Journaling compels you to become more specific with your generalized thoughts and feelings. This is not to suggest that a page full of words perfectly represents what's happening on the inside. That would be foolish. But journaling can move you closer to understanding more about yourself.

Reflection and Examination

With journaling, once you recognize what you're to write about, you can then con-

sider its value. You can write about your feelings, your situations, how you respond-
ed to events. You can reflect and answer questions like these:

- Was that the right response?
- What were my other options?
- Did I lose control and act impulsively?
- If this happened again, should I do the same thing? Would I do the same thing?
- How can I be different as a result of this situation?

Spiritual Insights

One of the main goals of journaling is to learn new spiritual insights about God,
yourself, and the world. When you take time to journal, you have the opportunity to
pause and consider how God is working in your life and in the lives of those
around you, so you don't miss the work he's accomplishing. And journaling helps
you remember.

What to Write

There isn't one way to journal, no set number of times per week, no rules for the
length of each journal entry. Figure out what works best for you. Get started with
these options:

A letter or prayer to God
Many Christians struggle with maintaining a consistent prayer life. Writing
out your prayers can help strengthen it. Begin with this question: *What do I
want to tell God right now?*

A letter to or a conversation with another person
Sometimes conversations with others can be difficult because we're not sure
what we ought to say. Have you ever walked away from an interaction and
20 minutes later think, *I should have said…?* Journaling conversations
before they happen can help you think through the issues and be intentional in your interactions with others. As a result, you can feel confident as
you begin your conversations because you've taken time to consider the
issues.

Conflict and pain
You may find it helpful to write about your conflicts with others, especially
those that take you by surprise. By journaling soon after, you can reflect

and learn from the conflicts. You'll be better prepared for the next time you face a similar situation. Conflicts are generally difficult to navigate. Thinking through the interactions typically yields helpful personal insights.

When you're experiencing pain is a good time to settle your thoughts and consider the nature of your feelings. The great thing about exploring your feelings is that you're only accountable to God. You don't have to worry about hurting anyone's feelings by what you write in your journal (if you keep it private).

Personal motivation
The Bible is clear regarding two heart truths:

- How you act is a reflection of who you are on the inside (Luke 6:45).
- You can take the right action for the wrong reason (James 4:3).

The condition of your heart is so important. Molding your motives to God's desire is central to being a follower of Christ. The Pharisees did many of the right things, but for the wrong reasons. Reflect on the *real* reasons you do what you do.

Personal Impact
Have you ever gone to bed thinking, *That was a mistake. I didn't intend for that to happen!*? Probably! No one is perfect. You can't predict all of the consequences of your actions. Reflecting on how your actions impact others will help you relate better to others.

God's work in your life
If you write in your journal in the evening, you can answer this question: *What did God teach me today?*

If you journal in the morning, you can answer this question: *God, what were you trying to teach me yesterday that I missed?* When you reflect on yesterday's events, you may find a common theme that God may have been weaving into your life during the day, one you missed because you were busy. When you see God's hand in your life, even a day later, you know God loves you and is guiding you.

Scripture
Journal about whatever you learn from the Bible. Rewrite a verse in your own words, or figure out how a passage is structured. Try to uncover the key truths from the verses and figure out how the verses apply to your life.

SCRIBBLES

SCRBBLES

JOURNALING page

the southern bound-dry, 1988
eater bar

Thug ... the sap who warried the sad
Whe ... eded the shet
And ... aught from the rat
Whe ... the drug
The ... the radde the ... but
Thi ... ...
Wh ... the sap

finest

SCRIBBLES

This is the house that Jack
This is the maiden all forlorn
Who milked her baby yet
By the tattered man who
Who killed the cat
When
And bought from the rat
That lay in the house that

SCRIBBLES

SCRIBBLES

JOURNALING page

par

SCRIBBLES

SCRIBBLES

finest

SCRIBBLES

SCRIBBLES

SCRIBBLES

SCRIBBLES

PRAYING IN YOUR SMALL GROUP

As believers, we're called to support one another in prayer, and prayer should become a consistent part of creating a healthy small group.

One of the purposes of prayer is to align our hearts with God's. By doing this, we can more easily think his thoughts and feel his feelings—in our limited human way. Prayer shouldn't be a how-well-did-I-do performance or a self-conscious, put-on-the-spot task to fear. Your small group may need time to get comfortable with praying out loud. That's okay.

Follow Jesus' Example

When you do pray, silently or aloud, follow the practical, simple words of Jesus in Matthew 6.

Pray sincerely.

"And when you pray, do not be like the hypocrites, for they love to pray standing in the synagogues and on the street corners to be seen by men. I tell you the truth, they have received their reward in full."

—Matthew 6:5

In the Old Testament, God's people were disciplined prayer warriors. They developed specific prayers to use for every special occasion or need. They had prayers for light and darkness, prayers for fire and rain, prayers for good news and bad. They even had prayers for travel, holidays, holy days, and Sabbath days.

Every day the faithful would stop to pray at 9:00 A.M., noon, and 3:00 P.M., a sort of religious coffee break. Their ritual was impressive, to say the least, but being legalistic has its downside. The proud, self-righteous types would strategically plan their schedules to be in the middle of a crowd when it was time for prayer so everyone could hear them as they prayed loudly. You can see the problem. What was intended to promote spiritual passion became a drama for the crowd.

The Lord wants our prayers addressed to him alone. That seems obvious enough, yet how many of us pray more with the need to impress our listeners than to communicate with God? This is the problem if you're prideful like the Pharisees about the excellent quality of your prayers. But it can also be a problem if you're new to prayer and concerned that you don't know how to "pray right." Don't concern yourself with what others think; just talk to God as if you were sitting in a chair next to him.

Pray simply.

"And when you pray, do not keep on babbling like pagans, for they think they will be heard because of their many words. Do not be like them, for your Father knows what you need before you ask him."

—Matthew 6:7-8

The Lord doesn't ask to be dazzled with brilliantly crafted language. Nor is he impressed with lengthy monologues. It's freeing to know that he wants us to keep it simple.

Pray specifically.

"This, then, is how you should pray: 'Our Father in heaven, hallowed be your name, your kingdom come, your will be done on earth as it is in heaven. Give us today our daily bread. Forgive us our debts, as we also have forgiven our debtors. And lead us not into temptation, but deliver us from the evil one.'"

—Matthew 6:9-13

What the church has come to call **The Lord's Prayer** is a model of the kind of brief but specific prayers we may offer anytime, anywhere. Look at some of the specific items mentioned:

Adoration—hallowed be your name

Provision—your kingdom come...your will be done...give us today our daily bread

Forgiveness—forgive us our debts

Protection—lead us not into temptation

PRAYER REQUEST GUIDELINES

Because prayer time is so vital, small group members need to know some basic guidelines for sharing, handling, and praying for prayer requests. Without a commitment from each person to honor these simple suggestions, prayer time can be dominated by one person, be a gossipfest, or be a never-ending story time. (There are appropriate times to tell personal stories, but this may not be the best time.)

Here are a few suggestions for each group to consider:

Write the requests down.

Each small group member should write down every prayer request on the **Prayer Request Log** (pages 132-137). When you commit to a small group, you're agreeing to be part of the spiritual community, which includes praying for one another. By keeping track of prayer requests, you can be aware of how God answers them. You'll be amazed at God's power and faithfulness.

As an alternative, one person can record the requests and e-mail them to the rest of the group. If your group chooses this option, *safeguard confidentiality.* Be sure personal information isn't compromised. Some people share e-mail accounts with parents or siblings. Develop a workable plan for this option.

Give everyone an opportunity to share.

As a group, be mindful of the amount of time remaining and the number of people who still want to share. You won't be able to share every thought or detail about a situation.

Obviously if someone experiences a crisis, you may need to focus exclusively on that group member by giving him or her extended time and focused prayer. (However, *true* crises are infrequent.)

The leader can limit the time by making a comment such as one of the following:

- Everyone can share one praise or request.
- Simply tell us what to pray for. We can talk more later.
- We're only going to pray for requests about the people in our group.
- We've run out of time to share prayer requests. Take a moment to write down your prayer request and give it to me [or identify another person]. You'll get them by e-mail tomorrow.

Just as people are free to share, they're free to not share.

The goal of a healthy small group should be to create an environment where participants feel comfortable sharing about their lives. Still, not everyone needs to share each week. Here's what I tell my small group:

> As a small group we're here to support one another in prayer. This doesn't mean that everyone has to share something. In fact, I don't want you to think, *I've got to share something*. There's no need to make up prayer requests just to have something to say. If you have something you'd like the group to pray for, let us know. If not, that's fine too.

No gossip allowed.

Don't allow sharing prayer requests to become an excuse for gossip. This is easy to do if you all aren't careful. If you're not part of the problem or solution, consider the information gossip. Sharing the request without the story behind it helps prevent gossip. Also speak in general terms without giving names or details ("I have a friend who's in trouble. God knows who it is. Pray for me that I can be a good friend.").

If a prayer request starts going astray, someone should kindly intercede, perhaps with a question such as, "How can we pray for *you* in this situation?"

Don't give advice or try to fix the problem.

When people share their struggles and problems, a common response is to try to fix the problem by offering advice. At the right time, the group might provide input on a particular problem, but during prayer time, keep focused on praying for the need. Often God's best work in a person's life comes through times of struggle and pain.

Keep in touch.

Make sure you exchange phone numbers and emails before you leave the first meeting, so you can contact someone who needs prayer or encouragement before the next time your group meets. You can write each person's contact information on the **Small Group Roster** (page 90).

During the Small Group Gathering

- One person closes in prayer for the entire group.
- Pray silently. Have one person close the silent prayer time after a while with *Amen.*
- The leader or other group member prays out loud for each person in the group.
- Everyone prays for one request or person. This can be done randomly during prayer or, as the request is shared, a willing pray-er can announce, "I'll pray for that."
- Everyone who wants to pray takes a turn or two. Not everyone needs to pray out loud.
- Split the group into half and pray together in a smaller group.
- Pair up and pray for each other.
- On occasion, each person can share what he or she is thankful for before a prayer request, so prayer requests don't become negative from focusing only on problems. Prayer isn't just asking for stuff. It includes praising God and being thankful for his generosity toward us.

STARTING to go where God wants you to be

■ If you're having an animated discussion about a Bible passage or a life situation, don't feel like you *must* cut it short for prayer requests. Use it as an opportunity to add a little variety to the prayer time by praying some *other* day between sessions.

Outside the Group Time

You can use these options if you run out of time to pray during the meeting or in addition to prayer during the meeting.

■ Send prayer requests to each other via e-mail.
■ Pick partners and phone each other.
■ Have each person in the small group choose a day to pray for everyone in the group. Perhaps you can work it out to have each day of the week covered. Let participants report back at each meeting for accountability.
■ Have each person pray for just one other person in the group for the entire week. (Everyone prays for the person on the left or on the right or draw names.)

PRAYER REQUEST LOG

DATE	who shared	ReQuest	rEsponse/anSweR

PRAYER REQUEST LOG

DATE	who shared	ReQuest	rEsponse/ anSweR

PRAYER REQUEST LOG

DATE	who shared	ReQuest	r8sponse/ anSweR

PRAYER REQUEST LOG

DATE	who shared	ReQuest	rEspOnse/anSweR

PRAYER REQUEST LOG

DATE	who shared	ReQuest	rEsponse/anSweR

PRAYER REQUEST LOG

DATE	who shared	ReQuest	rEsponse/ anSweR

LIFE TOGETHER FOR A YEAR

Y our group will benefit the most if you work through the entire LIFETOGETHER series. The longer your group is together, the better your chances of maturing spiritually and integrating the biblical purposes into your life. Here's a plan to complete the series in one year.

I recommend you begin with **STARTING to Go Where God Wants You to Be,** because it contains an introduction to each of the five biblical purposes (though it isn't mandatory). You can use the rest of the books in any order.

As you look at your youth ministry calendar, you may want to use the books in the order they complement events the youth group will be participating in. For example, if you plan to have an evangelism outreach in the fall, study **SHARING Your Story and God's Story** first to build momentum. Study **SERVING Others in Love** in late winter to prepare for the spring break missions' trip.

Use your imagination to celebrate the completion of each book. Have a worship service, an outreach party, a service project, a fun night out, a meet-the-family dinner, or whatever else you can dream up.

Number of weeks	Meeting topic
1	Planning meeting—a casual gathering to get acquainted, discuss expectations, and refine the covenant (see page 88).
6	**STARTING to Go Where God Wants You to Be**
1	Celebration
6	**CONNECTING Your Heart to Others'**
1	Celebration
6	**SHARING Your Story and God's Story**
1	Celebration
6	**GROWING to Be Like Jesus**
1	Celebration
6	**SERVING Others in Love**
1	Celebration
6	**SURRENDERING Your Life to Honor God**
1	Celebration
2	Christmas break
1	Easter break
6	Summer break
52	One year

Dear Kathleen,

I just wanted to let you know how thankful I am for the dedication you showed me as my small group leader. I love telling people, "Kathleen is my small group leader — she's the best!" Next to God, you have had the greatest influence in my life. I want to grow up and love people like you, love Jesus like you do, love my future husband like you do, and be a small group leader like you.

What's amazing about you, is that all the girls in our small group felt like you liked them the most. We also felt your push. As I look back over my junior high and high school years, you loved me enough to challenge me to change. Thank you for always asking about my prayer life, my quiet times, my ministry, my heart. Thanks for seeing who I could be.

You've made a huge difference in my life. Thank you!

Love,
Sarah

Whether you are a student or a leader, when you're a part of a small group — investing your life in others — you're making a difference that will last an eternity. At Simply Youth Ministry we are dedicated to helping you do just that. For students, we've got tools like the *One Minute Bible*, that will help you grow in your faith. For leaders, we've got all kinds of resources that will help you simplify your ministry and save you time. For both of you, we have a deep appreciation for your commitment to serving Christ and loving each other.

doug fields'
simply youth ministry
simplifying ministry...saving you time.

toll free: 1-866-9-simply
simplyyouthministry.com

ABOUT THE AUTHORS

Doug Fields, a respected youth ministry leader for over two decades, has authored or coauthored more than 30 books, including **Purpose-Driven Youth Ministry**, **Your First Two Years of Youth Ministry**, and **Videos That Teach**. With an M.Div. from Fuller Theological Seminary, Doug is the youth pastor at Saddleback Church, president of simplyyouthministry.com, and a frequent presenter at Youth Specialties events. Doug and his wife, Cathy, have three children.

Brett Eastman is pastor of membership and small groups at Saddleback Church, where there are now over 1,500 small group leaders and a growing network of volunteer coaches and bivocational pastors. Brett created the Healthy Small Group strategy and he leads the Large Church Small Group Forums for the Leadership Network. Brett is coauthor of the DOING LIFE TOGETHER Bible study series. Brett and his wife, Dee, have five children.